T0284291

The status quo is broken. Humanity today faces multiple interconnected challenges, some of which could prove existential. If we believe the world could be different, if we want it to be *better*, examining the purpose of what we do – and what is done in our name – is more pressing than ever.

The What Is It For? series examines the purpose of the most important aspects of our contemporary world, from religion and free speech to animal rights and the Olympics. It illuminates what these things are by looking closely at what they do.

The series offers fresh thinking on current debates that gets beyond the overheated polemics and easy polarizations. Across the series, leading experts explore new ways forward, enabling readers to engage with the possibility of real change.

Series editor: George Miller

Visit **bristoluniversitypress.co.uk/what-is-it-for** to find out more about the series.

**STEVE COOKE** is Associate Professor of Political Theory at the University of Leicester, where he researches animal ethics and political disobedience. He sits on the Research Advisory Committee of the Vegan Society and was previously Research Fellow of the Society for Applied Philosophy and the University of Manchester.

# WHAT ARE ANIMAL RIGHTS FOR?

STEVE COOKE

First published in Great Britain in 2023 by

Bristol University Press
University of Bristol
1–9 Old Park Hill
Bristol
BS2 8BB
UK
t: +44 (0)117 374 6645
e: bup-info@bristol.ac.uk

Details of international sales and distribution partners are available at
bristoluniversitypress.co.uk

British Library Cataloguing in Publication Data
A catalogue record for this book is available from the British Library

ISBN 978-1-5292-2841-0 paperback
ISBN 978-1-5292-2842-7 ePub
ISBN 978-1-5292-2843-4 ePdf

Cover design: Tom Appshaw
Bristol University Press uses environmentally
responsible print partners.
Printed and bound in Great Britain by CPI Group (UK) Ltd,
Croydon, CR0 4YY

To all the creatures who cannot speak for themselves, and to Tam: thank you for putting up with me, and for not pushing me down a well.

# CONTENTS

# LIST OF FIGURES AND BOXES

## Figures

## Boxes

# 1

# INTRODUCTION

In March 2020 animal rights campaign group Viva! conducted an undercover investigation into a UK pig farm near where I live. Thankfully, their investigation eventually led to the farm's closure. Flat House Farm housed more than 8,000 pigs in horrific conditions. Viva! video footage revealed agonized pigs, twitching and shivering as they lay dying in pens awash with faeces. Many animals were visibly starving, their ribs showing and their bellies distended. Often, pigs were so hungry they turned to cannibalism. Pigs were shown smeared in each other's blood, displaying large, infected wounds and prolapsed hernias. Throughout the five-minute video, pigs with severe untreated respiratory illnesses could be heard coughing. Hidden cameras captured farm workers bashing sick piglets to death on the bars of the crates their mothers were confined in. Meanwhile, feral cats devoured piglets beside their helpless mothers. Investigators found the bones of animals who had been left to rot in the stalls, and animals trampling one another in overcrowded conditions. Other footage showed farm workers using scissors, without anaesthetic, to cut tails from piglets, and pliers to clip their teeth. These practices are intended to reduce tail-biting in crowded conditions and are supposed to be done with pain relief.

Nearly twenty years before the Flat House Farm scandal, I watched similar undercover footage recorded in a slaughterhouse. That video, together with my own experiences on farms and my conversations with farm workers, activists and veterinary inspectors, prompted me to think again about how animals should be treated. The Viva! investigation into Flat House Farm occurred while the farm was certified by the UK's Red Tractor scheme. That scheme markets itself as ensuring that the UK is a world leader in pig (and other animal) welfare. In the years since the video that persuaded me to give up meat was filmed, little has changed besides an increase in the number and size of factory farms. Undercover investigations of farm and slaughterhouse conditions are common, and they all show the same things. Behind closed doors, animals are subjected to cruelty and brutality on an almost unimaginable scale. All of this occurs in a country that prides itself on its love for animals and its high welfare standards. Conditions in other countries are often even worse.

Imagine a different world. Imagine a future in which nonhuman animals can trust human beings. They can trust us not just because we have collectively decided that we ought not to harm them, but also because they have been granted rights. These rights are backed up by the threat of punishment by the state if we transgress. In this world, nonhuman animals are largely able to live without the risk of being killed, eaten or harmfully experimented on. So long as they present no immediate threat, animals are free from harm at human hands. The society I describe is very different from our own. Its people are almost entirely vegan. The food they eat, the products they use, their ways of living are very different from today's norm. Its people look back on today's treatment of nonhuman animals with a sense of disbelief and horror. This isn't a society without animals in it, however. In this future, nonhumans continue to live in mutually beneficial relationships with humans. Companion and working animals, such as guide and service dogs, remain. They live among us not as property, but as citizens, residents and employees. No longer are humans permitted to have a pet killed simply for convenience. Instead, those animals who live among us have rights to representation in parliament; their interests are considered in urban planning; they have rights to time off, medical care and retirement benefits. Where they work, it is because it can be shown that they do so in roles they enjoy and that benefit them. Farms no longer breed, kill and exploit animals; zoos house far fewer individual animals, with a more restricted range of species; and scientific research is conducted using technology that does not rely on animal testing. In short, this imagined future is one where animals are treated as our fellows, not as mere instruments for our use.

This, I think, is the future that we ought to work towards. In this book, I try to explain why I think this and describe some of the problems – both moral and practical – that stand in the way. Even if you do not end up agreeing with me, I hope that you will at least come away understanding the force of the animal rights position as well as some of its potential weaknesses.

To achieve this, I begin by providing some historical context about the way that nonhuman animals have been used by humans, and the cultural attitudes surrounding these uses. After this, I explain how the concept of sentience gives us reason to be concerned, from an ethical point of view, about the treatment of other animals.

In Chapter 2, I trace the history of animal rights as an idea, using some of the historical debates to introduce important moral theories and areas of disagreement. Knowledge of these theories and arguments lays the ground for a discussion in Chapter 3 about the theory of rights, and the connection between rights, justice and political morality. That chapter will do some of the most important work in explaining why nonhuman animals ought to be granted rights.

In Chapters 4 and 5, I set out what animal rights would mean for some of the common ways we make use of nonhuman animals: as food and for materials; as entertainment; for companionship; and for research. I also introduce some interesting new areas that push the boundaries of animal rights theory: the possibility that crustaceans and insects might be owed rights;

the idea of nonhumans as citizens; and problems with assigning rights to wild animals. Chapter 6 describes the social and psychological hurdles that must be overcome before justice for nonhuman animals can be achieved. That chapter explains how the concept of rights functions in moral reasoning and how it can serve as the focus for social movements. Towards the end of the chapter, I highlight some criticisms of the concept of rights as well as replies to those critiques. Finally, in Chapter 7, I go beyond the idea of rights. That chapter will argue that the imagined future I have just described is more likely to occur and would be better if the people who live in it adopt attitudes of respect, openness and trustworthiness towards nonhuman animals. Let us begin with a little historical context before tackling the ethical issues.

Humans have been using nonhuman animals for a very long time: the first to be domesticated were probably wolves, roughly fifteen thousand years ago in the Palaeolithic era. We have been farming sheep, goats, pigs and cattle for ten to eleven thousand years.[1] The process of domestication involved keeping animals in captivity, habituating them to human contact and selective breeding to eliminate behavioural traits thought undesirable. After thousands of years, animals farmed or kept as companions today are unlike those they are descended from. In the UK there exists a herd of wild cattle that has been kept genetically isolated for hundreds of years. Although these Chillingham cattle are descended from domesticated breeds, they are untamed and quite different from modern farmed varieties. The Chillingham cattle are smaller,[2] more aggressive, noisy and territorial than those farmed today for meat or milk. Farming, particularly industrialized farming, requires large numbers of animals to live in confined spaces and respond calmly to handling. Modern animals, particularly those reared for food, have therefore been selected and bred for their sociability, docility, vulnerability and for features that make the products derived from their bodies efficient to produce and desirable to own or consume. Let's look at these processes in more detail.

Farming as we know it today started to take shape in the eighteenth century. From the end of that century rapid population growth in Europe, together with increased demand for food, resulted in the intensification of animal agriculture. These changes were accompanied by industrialization and urbanization. Developing trade and transport infrastructure helped create a transnational trade in livestock and meat, leading to networks of meat-based economic interdependence.[3]

In the late eighteenth and early nineteenth centuries, the spirit of scientific discovery also resulted in an expansion of vivisection, the process of performing operations on living animals for research or demonstration purposes. Animal experimentation became established as part of the scientific method in medicine. One of the pioneers of scientific physiology, Claude Bernard (1813–78), stated, 'experiments on animals are entirely conducive for the toxicology and hygiene of man. The effects of these substances are the same on man as on animals, save for differences in degree.'[4] There was also a belief that exposure to the suffering of animals during vivisection would help students become inured to the pain suffered by their human patients.[5]

This period witnessed a transformation in medicine, with numerous medical advances and the spread of hospitals. Scientific methods were deployed in the service of understanding disease and physiology, which resulted in a rise in experimentation. To reduce risks in clinical trials, increasing use was made of animals as analogues for humans. From the 1870s came growing public concern over the cruelty of vivisection and the growth of animal welfare movements and organizations. Many tried to push back against industrialization and the growing prevalence of the scientific, rationalistic worldview. Technological advances threatened rapid, frightening change and a reconfiguration of the relationship between humans, nature and other animals. Campaigners worried that science risked disordering harmonious relationships with the natural world.[6]

In the nineteenth century, change intensified. Towards the end of the century, aided by developments in transport and refrigeration, the American meat industry had become centralized and developed industrialized slaughter and meat-packing processes. In the twentieth century, management practices further intensified, and the 1930s saw the introduction in the US of the first battery farms for poultry and automated slaughter systems for pigs. The 1930s also witnessed the infamous sulfanilamide disaster. In 1937 a US pharmaceutical company widely distributed a treatment for streptococcal infections in a new liquid form, resulting in the deaths of over one hundred patients. The disaster resulted in the American Food and Drug Administration passing a law requiring animal testing for food, medicine and cosmetics.

After the Second World War came yet more transformation. Increased use of automation enabled highly intensive farming and less reliance on human labour. Automation was made possible, in part, by the connection of farms to new national electricity grids, which also provided artificial light and greater temperature control. In the 1950s geneticists began creating more productive hybrid strains of chickens. Meanwhile, advances in plant-based agriculture created a huge growth in animal-feed production, helping producers to meet ever-growing demand for meat. Medical advances resulting from the discovery of penicillin in 1928 and the development of further antibiotics through the 1940s and 1950s enabled animals to be kept in greater numbers and with closer housing.

Today, most farmed animals are housed in small spaces and in large groups. Access to light, space, food and company is carefully regulated. They have been bred to grow more quickly and produce more muscle mass, milk or eggs than their predecessors. Feeding is automated, and feed has been carefully formulated to encourage rapid growth. Enhanced production is enabled by medical technology such as vaccines, artificial insemination, hormones and antibiotics. On the consumer side, expectations that meat should be the centrepiece of a meal, together with demands for readily available, cheap meat, have exacerbated these trends. Farming practices have shifted to specialize in monocultures, where only a single species is farmed in each unit or location. Sometimes this covers only one phase of an animal's life, and it is usually dedicated to the production of specific products, such as eggs, dairy or certain kinds of meat. Farms today are much larger and fewer and are often owned by large corporations. The result is suffering and death on a far greater scale than at any other period in history. Simultaneously, tens of millions of animals are bred for scientific experiments.

Thousands of years of animal agriculture have left the use of animal bodies deeply embedded in our cultures. Animal products are used either as an ingredient or in the manufacture of products as wide-ranging as toilet paper, bank notes, paints and pigments, sugar, fabrics, food, medicines, fuel, fertilizers, brushes, varnish, pottery, beer and wine, and contraceptives. Animal bodies are used and regarded in much the same way as plants – as renewable resources or mere things. The scale of this use is staggering: worldwide, tens of millions of animals are slaughtered every day, hundreds of billions per year. So many fish are killed that their deaths are estimated in billions of tonnes rather than numbers of individual creatures. In April 2022 alone, the United States Department of Agriculture (USDA) reported that 2,813,4000 cattle were slaughtered in the US. Rearing this many animals requires one-third of the world's grain production and more than three-quarters of soy production. In all, nearly 80 per cent of agricultural land is used to support animal agriculture. Imagine that humanity one day creates a true Artificial Intelligence (AI), endowed with its own sense of morality, and that we show it the figures for daily animal slaughter, show it how we use corpses for comfort, enjoyment and convenience. No doubt, the AI would be appalled. It might ask us to explain why we do such a thing and how our societies ended up like this. What would we say to it? How would we explain?

One explanation is that our societies view animals through an anthropocentric lens. Anthropocentrism is the belief that humans are either the most important or the only entities that matter. Anthropocentric views either completely discount the idea that nonhuman animals matter, or they assign lesser weight to animal lives and interests than to those of humans. Such views are common for many reasons; one is that some of the world's biggest religions make metaphysical claims about the superiority of humans. That means that they believe human superiority to be a law built into the very fabric of the universe. For example, the Christian Bible reports God as having told humankind: 'Fill the earth and subdue it, have dominion over the fish in the sea, the birds of the air and every living thing that moves on the earth.'[7] Meanwhile, the Qur'an instructs Muslims that nonhuman animals have been provided for human use:

> It is Allah Who has made cattle for you, that you may ride
> on some of them, and eat of some of them. And you have
> other advantages in them, and that, by means of them, you
> may satisfy any desire that there may be in your breasts.
> And on them and on ships are you borne.[8]

These views see humans as special, and nature as having been created for us to use and enjoy. Associated with these beliefs is not just a hierarchical attitude, but a model of interaction based on ruling (dominion) or stewardship. If stewardship approaches presume the death of an animal to be bad, it is because it deprives a human of something they value or depend upon. For example, in conservation this approach translates into protecting species and habitats because humans enjoy them. Concern for nature is not because nature is sacred or valuable for its own sake, but because we owe it to other humans.

The idea that nonhuman animals exist for our use is also used to justify their status as property. The law regards most of the animals we interact with as property. In contemporary legal systems, the world is usually divided into persons and things, a distinction dating all the way back to Roman law. Persons have rights and legal standing, things do not. Things can be owned, persons cannot. This division into persons and things means that nonhuman animals inhabit much the same space in law as sofas, TVs, chairs, paintings and so on. Ownership rights allow the possessor of an animal to use, trade or destroy it with only limited constraints. Unowned animals – those that live wild, or free-roaming animals – are not persons but merely things that have not had a legitimate ownership claim made over them.

As well as the conceptual status of nonhuman animals as property or things that exist for our use, there are several historical and structural explanations for their treatment. One of those is that animal agriculture is hugely profitable and woven into the fabric of our economies. Not only that, but the use of animals as beasts of burden, forms of transport and sources of products has been vital to economic growth and to key events in history. Today, animal agriculture generates vast wealth for powerful individuals and companies. It also supports huge numbers of jobs and secondary businesses. Modern animal agriculture is heavily industrialized and often involves vast corporate farms. These mega-farms process gigantic herds and flocks of animals. The Mudanjiang City Mega Farm in China has a hundred thousand dairy cows. Another farm in Saudi Arabia produces around a billion litres of milk from forty-seven thousand cows. Farms with herds numbering tens of thousands are increasingly common around the world. These farms rely on highly mechanized and automated processes to function and the farmers who own them have wealth measured in billions of dollars. As a result, the profit motive for promoting the use of nonhuman animals as products should not be underestimated. All those features of modern farming make it a significant part of contemporary economic systems, around which so much else of our ways of living is organized.

One of the ways that the economic importance of animal products manifests in cultural attitudes is via their association with luxury, comfort and wealth. Leather goods command a premium and mark out products, such as cars and clothing, that use them as desirable luxuries. Animal products also have a range of other positive cultural associations. Animals are consumed to celebrate moments of significance such as Thanksgiving, Christmas, Muharram or Shavuot. Consumption of meat and dairy is associated with health, enjoyment, wellbeing, status and identity. For example, products such as steak are associated with masculinity, and various animal products feature in items or dishes connected with national, regional or ethnic identity. Because these things are so important to our sense of self and our view of our place in the world, and because the associations are positive, it is hard to imagine life without them. Opposition to the use of animal products is thus resisted on many fronts, and the scale of use has ironically helped normalize that use.

## Sentience

Despite the importance of animal production, consumption and exploitation to our history and cultures, many people are ethically troubled by the way animals are treated. Some are concerned about the serious threat posed by animal agriculture to the environment. For others, such as Jains, their concern is a spiritual or religious objection to violence. But for an increasing number, it is because they believe that nonhuman animals have rights, and that the way we treat them commonly violates those rights.

Many people think that the reason animals should have rights is because they are sentient. Sentience describes the capacity to feel. Sentient beings experience positive and negative mental states. Another way to describe this is to say that sentient beings are conscious; they experience the world in ways that are either pleasant or unpleasant. Sentient beings can have feelings like pain and pleasure, happiness, fear, joy, suffering, anger, frustration and perhaps even complex emotions like trust, envy or love. From the earliest days of the animal welfare movement in the eighteenth century, the capacity of sentience has played a key role. Writing in 1767 the British politician James Burgh described the capacity of animals to feel and think: 'an animal can feel, though it cannot complain'.[9] Later, veterinarian William Youatt wrote:

> we should never forget that the animal over which we exercise our power has all the organs which render it susceptible of pleasure and of pain. It sees, it hears, it smells, it tastes. It feels with acuteness. How mercifully, then, ought we to exercise the dominion entrusted to our care![10]

Awareness of other animals' capacity to feel has been known about for thousands of years even if it has not always been accorded much moral significance. Nevertheless, knowing that other animals feel pain like us has galvanized numerous animal protection movements. These grew to prominence in nineteenth-century Britain, helping to create several early anti-cruelty laws and campaigning societies. The first animal protection group was the Society for the Prevention of Cruelty to Animals, created in 1824 to make sure that an 1822 law protecting draft and farm animals was enforced. Other organizations formed to campaign on specific issues, such as the suffering caused by vivisection. Pressure from these groups resulted in the 1875 creation of a royal commission on vivisection, which in turn led to the Cruelty to Animals Act 1876, known also as the Vivisection Act. The Act mandated that vivisection be performed only for an original, useful purpose.

It is the capacity for sentience that underpins much animal protection legislation and the science of animal welfare. Sentience is put forward as the primary reason why we ought to care about nonhuman animals for their own sakes and why we ought to grant them rights. Many ethical arguments about the treatment of nonhuman animals focus on showing that they can and do feel pain. For example, campaigns to improve the treatment of fish began with attempts to prove sentience. Likewise, arguments against battery farming tried to show that close confinement caused hens suffering. Sentience and the feelings associated with it are the primary elements of animal wellbeing or welfare.

An important debate in ethics and welfare science concerns the different ways in which animals are sentient and whether the strength and complexity of their feelings vary by species. If a being can experience more complex emotions, or if it experiences pain or pleasure more intensely, then we will have reasons to treat it differently from one that does not, or that only feels them faintly. Similarly, we might assess the status of a being that can feel pain but not pleasure differently from one that feels only pleasure. While these are hypothetical examples, consideration has been given to using genetic engineering to eliminate animals' capacity to feel pain. These variations can cause animal rights theorists to struggle when it comes to explaining the relationship between sentience and political or moral equality. If rights protect sentience, and sentience comes in degrees, then it appears to follow that rights should vary in strength. For example, a chimpanzee's capacity to feel fear or pain might be much greater than that of a frog or lobster, giving the chimpanzee stronger rights against suffering. Similarly, some animals, such as elephants, pigs and dolphins, have a much stronger and persistent sense of self than others (see discussion of the mirror test in Chapter 4), making death worse for them than for simpler creatures.

In one sense, this is very counter-intuitive and can lead to conclusions most of us would rather not face because sentience also varies among humans. One solution is to say that merely reaching a certain threshold of sentience is enough to grant rights and that any variation above that isn't relevant to rights. Along these lines, the Australian philosopher Peter Singer has argued that we shouldn't focus on differences in capacities and that treating people as equals requires giving their interests and needs equal consideration (more on Singer later).[11]

Another is to accept rights of different strengths. This route is not as bad as it may first seem because it only comes into play when there is a clash of rights – it would not permit the violation of weaker rights merely so that those with stronger rights can gain some benefit. Nevertheless, that conclusion would be unpalatable to most. Others think talk of degrees of sentience is misguided. Perhaps we ought to regard sentience as something that is present in different configurations rather than different degrees. While this view appears to escape the problem, pointing instead to different sets of rights, it still seems likely that comparative evaluations of different capacities will sometimes be necessary for moral judgements.

Those problems aside, if a species is established to be sentient, then this is usually taken as sufficient justification to grant members of that species legal protections. For example, the first modern animal protection law made it illegal to cause or permit unnecessary suffering.[12] More recent laws explicitly refer to 'the welfare of animals as sentient beings'.[13] Sentience is particularly important to understanding animal rights because it describes what it is like for an individual being from its own perspective. Hence it forms a justification for laws that protect individual creatures rather than populations, species, ecosystems or communities. We will return to this topic in later chapters.

# 2

# A BRIEF INTELLECTUAL HISTORY OF ANIMAL RIGHTS

Now that we have some background, it's time to consider animal rights in more detail. Rights describe entitlements to things or protection from certain treatment. The fundamental idea that nonhuman animals are owed rights seems simple. Indeed, we might even look at legal systems that prohibit cruelty to animals and conclude from these that they already possess rights. Unfortunately, the picture is more complicated than it first appears. Although nonhuman animals seem to possess all sorts of legal rights, these aren't strong enough to offer the kinds of protections animal rights activists have in mind. For example, laws that protect nonhuman animals against 'unnecessary suffering' depend on a peculiar idea of necessity that is only partly determined by the animal's interests. In human cases, by contrast, rights are thought to protect individuals from being used to promote social goods. Those rights are justified in terms of the inherent worth of every human being.

In the nonhuman case, rights against suffering only require that people balance the animal's interests against other benefits. Rights against unnecessary suffering merely mean that animal suffering must be proportionate to the aims that cause the suffering. Thus, hunting an animal must not cause it more suffering than is needed for the hunt to succeed, but hunting is not forbidden, even if it inevitably causes some suffering. Similarly, laws which say that scientific procedures must not cause unnecessary suffering don't prohibit procedures that cause unavoidable suffering. In the same way, laws against killing animals are rarely intended only to protect an animal for the animal's own sake. A pet owner or farmer may kill their animal almost on a whim so long as the killing is done using legal methods. Laws against killing animals exist to prevent non-owners from damaging the property of others, or to maintain species or populations so that they can continued to be enjoyed by others. Additionally, the kind of protections nonhuman animals have aren't really possessed by them. A legal claim cannot be made on behalf of an animal; it can only be made about the treatment of the animal. This is because nonhuman animals lack *legal personhood* (more on this in Chapter 4).

By contrast, when we think about human rights against cruel and inhuman treatment, we regard these as being held by the person and as very stringent rules indeed. Human rights law doesn't permit torture as long as it stays within certain limits or allow it in exceptional circumstances; it forbids it altogether. Campaigners want the same sorts of rights for nonhuman animals. If nonhuman animals were granted such rights, they would have similar sorts of protections as those provided by human rights. Indeed, as we shall see later in this chapter, many theorists argue that the reasons nonhuman animals ought to have rights are the same as those for granting them to humans. The key feature that human and animal rights share is that they are both ways of talking about moral rights. The claim that nonhuman animals have *rights* is actually a claim that they have *moral rights*, and it has important theoretical and legal implications. To understand it, we need to spend a little time getting to grips with the concept of moral rights and its relationship with legal rights.

Once you start thinking about moral rights, you quickly realize that they are surprisingly difficult to understand and even more difficult to describe. Many people find the concept of a moral right both frustrating and baffling. They wonder where these rights come from, who came up with them, and what authority they have. We shan't get into the source of morality here, partly because to do so would make things unnecessarily complicated. However, for the idea of moral rights to get off the ground, we must make some assumptions. One is that moral claims are intelligible and capable of being true or false.

Fortunately, most of us behave as if it makes sense to say that certain acts are morally right or wrong;

good or bad; forbidden or permissible; praiseworthy or blameworthy. Most of us believe that when someone makes a claim such as 'torturing kittens for fun is wrong' then they are either correct or mistaken. If someone claims that torturing kittens for fun is not morally wrong, then the rest of us are likely to think they have made a serious error. (We will probably also want to keep a very careful eye on them.) Those who reject the idea that moral claims are meaningful, or that moral claims cannot be true or false, are few and this book isn't really for them.

Assuming that moral claims can intelligibly be made, how should we understand moral rights? First, to assert a moral right for yourself or others is to claim that there are strong moral reasons for the right-holder to be treated in a particular way. There are several ways we can think about what this means and how rights function in practice, and theorists often disagree. Some think of moral rights as rules that trump other sorts of considerations, much like trump cards in certain card games. For example, politeness or efficiency might be good reasons to act in a certain way, but they are overridden (trumped) by rights claims. We shouldn't stop to be polite while rushing to urgently save a life – life trumps politeness. The only thing that might trump a right is a more important right. For example, the right to life might trump a property right.

Others think that rights represent reasons that exclude other factors from being considerations at all. If someone is drowning and has a right to our assistance, it doesn't make to sense to balance their right against the economic value of the shoes we will ruin by saving them. The value of our shoes shouldn't even enter our thoughts; it ought not be a consideration at all. Alternatively, we can simply think of rights as very weighty moral considerations against which all sorts of other (moral and non-moral) considerations must be balanced. Whichever view you take, moral rights have a special importance compared with other sorts of reasons for action or inaction.

Aside from providing very strong moral reasons for acting or not acting, moral rights are universal and enforceable. This means, first, that they hold for everyone; they are universal, not relative. So, a claim like 'slavery is wrong' doesn't just mean that I shouldn't practise slavery; it means nobody should practise slavery. Not only that, but it also means that slavery was wrong in the past and will be wrong in the future. Second, moral rights are thought to be so important that people ought to be required to respect them. In other words, coercing people to respect the moral principle embodied in the right is morally permissible. So, asserting a right often functions as a claim that the law ought to require that the right be recognized and upheld. In this way, moral rights are claims about what laws there would be in ideal circumstances. As we shall see later, this makes moral rights strongly connected with the idea of justice.

Despite the link between moral and legal rights, we need to be careful not to treat them as the same. For one thing, many legal rights represent, or have represented, violations of moral rights. Laws that permitted slavery, or that treat women as inferior to men, or that embody racial hierarchies are all examples of immoral laws. Each of those laws has historically been grounded in false and biased claims about the different moral worth of people based on their sex or race. Other legal rights do not rely on moral claims at all for their justification. For example, many legal rights are the product of historical accident and exist only to preserve a status quo. The UK's monarch, for instance, has a property right to the carcasses of beached whales on British shores. Others relate to particular roles rather than being derived from universal moral principles. For example, it used to be the case in some countries that members of the clergy accused of a crime had a right to be tried in an ecclesiastical court under canon law rather than in a secular court. Similarly, members of the armed services today are tried for criminal offences in military courts.

These sorts of rights are different from the kinds of rights campaigners seek for nonhumans. Animal rights campaigners instead call for laws that recognize claims that hold wherever and whenever a being exists, and that protect a being's vital interests. These are often also called natural rights because they describe rights that don't depend on laws or customs; in that regard, they are pre-political. The commonest sorts of these claims are that nonhuman animals have rights not to be killed or made to suffer. When animal rights theorists argue for a moral right against suffering or death, what they mean is that the law should prevent people from killing or causing suffering even when doing so serves a human interest. Such rights ought to prevent one being's vital interests from being overridden to serve the interests of another.

We will discuss the relationship between rights and interests in more detail in the next chapter, but for now it will be helpful to explore how the idea of animal rights has developed. Aside from being very interesting, the intellectual history of animal rights is also helpful for illustrating some of the key philosophical debates and theoretical positions.

There is a long history of people, groups and movements opposing the killing of nonhuman animals and arguing that animals ought to be treated with kindness. Hinduism, Jainism and Buddhism all contain similar strictures against violence towards living things. For example, the ancient Indian philosopher Tiruvalluvar included a section on vegetarianism in the *Tirukkuṛaḷ* (commonly known as the *Kural*). This section has ten couplets against eating meat for the sake of kindness and purity. Tiruvalluvar claimed that eating meat hardens the heart and promotes violence: 'Like a man armed to kill, A meat-eater does not discriminate. Grace is not killing, to kill disgrace; And to eat a thing killed, profitless sin.' The *Kural* was written between the second century BCE and the eighth century CE.

The earliest recorded vegan was the eleventh-century Syrian poet, writer and philosopher Abu 'L'Ala Ahmad ibn 'Abdallah al-Ma'arrī, more commonly known as al-Ma'arrī. Although rendered blind by smallpox, al-Ma'arrī travelled widely in Syria and achieved considerable fame as a poet and thinker. Al-Ma'arrī is interesting for several reasons. One is that, although clearly influenced by Islam, and perhaps also by a vegetarian Christian sect,[1] his worldview is secular and grounded in reason. Indeed, he refers to Plato and Aristotle to praise (probably sarcastically) the arguments of an interlocutor. The second reason is that his writings show direct concern for nonhuman

**Box 2.1: From al-Ma'arrī's poem**

Come to me, that thou mayst hear the tidings of sound truth.

Do not unjustly eat what the water has given up, and do not desire as food the flesh of slaughtered animals,

Or the white (milk) of mothers who intended its pure draught for their young, not for noble ladies.

And do not grieve the unsuspecting birds by taking their eggs; for injustice is the worst of crimes.

And spare the honey which the bees get betimes by their industry from the flowers of fragrant plants;

For they did not store it that it might belong to others, nor did they gather it for bounty and gifts.

I washed my hands of all this; and would that I had perceived my way ere my temples grew hoar!...[2]

animals. Al-Ma'arrī is critical of animal cruelty and exploitation throughout his writings. However, the most important of his works concerning nonhuman animals is an exchange of letters, from around 1046 CE, with the Shi'ite missionary al-Mu'ayyad fī l-Dīn al-Shīrāzī. In the letters, al-Mu'ayyad asks for an explanation of a poem in which al-Ma'arrī argues against the use of animal products. The poem characterizes the consumption of eggs, honey and milk as theft and urges against eating flesh.

Much of the correspondence appears to be an attempt by al-Mu'ayyad to entrap al-Ma'arrī into admitting the crime of atheism and al-Ma'arrī's attempt to avoid

**Figure 2.1: Al-Ma'arrī**

The Syrian poet and philosopher al-Ma'arrī (973–1058 CE) is thought to be the first recorded vegan who chose this way of life on ethical grounds.

the charge. As a result, many of al-Ma'arrī's answers are theological, or refer to the cost and health benefits of veganism. However, he also makes some familiar ethical arguments. For example, he writes: 'The animals are, as you know, sensitive, and feel pain',[3] and he encourages sensitivity towards beings who feel pain, adding 'meat cannot be procured without infliction of pain on animals'.[4]

Even before al-Ma'arrī, we can find numerous influences on the modern animal rights tradition, particularly in ancient Greek thought. The earliest of these was Pythagoras, a philosopher whose name frequently begins histories of vegetarianism. Indeed, before the term 'vegetarian' was coined,[5] people often referred to it as a Pythagorean diet. For example, we find Antonio Cocci's *The Pythagorean Diet, of Vegetables Only, Conducive to the Preservation of Health, and the Cure of Diseases*, published in 1743, which describes:

> the free and universal use of every thing that is vegetable, tender and fresh, which requires little or no preparation to make it fit to eat, such as roots, leaves, flowers, fruits and feeds: and in a general abstinence from every thing that is animal, whether it be fresh or dried. Bird, Beast, or Fish.[6]

Pythagoras lived from around 570 to 490 BCE, and everything we know about him has been pieced together from accounts written by others. Despite this, and although he wasn't a vegetarian himself, he has been an influential figure to the vegetarian movement.

For Pythagoras, diet was about maintaining a healthy body, pure soul and peaceful character. He believed that after death human souls may sometimes inhabit the body of other animals. As a result, eating animals risked consuming a fellow human. In this respect, his beliefs were similar to the principle of *ahimsa* found in Jainism, Hinduism and Buddhism, which holds that harming other living beings damages one's soul. All these reasons make abstinence from animal products about the benefit to humans. Cocci's book was written for the purpose of improving human health rather than promoting animal rights. In other words, their reasons were anthropocentric, which makes them quite different from the claims al-Ma'arrī makes about pain and exploitation.

More promising ethical arguments can be found in the works of later thinkers in the Hellenistic period. For example, following Pythagoras, we find interesting claims attributed to the poet Empedocles, who lived from around 490 to 430 BCE in the Greek colony of Agrigentum on the island of Sicily. Like Pythagoras' work, much of Empedocles' writing has been lost. However, the Roman politician and philosopher Cicero (106–43 BCE) writes that 'Pythagoras and Empedocles (no average men, but thinkers of the greatest eminence) proclaim that all living creatures have the same standing in law', which some have translated as meaning that all living creatures are subject to the same principles of justice.[7] An earlier reference to Empedocles' writings exists in Aristotle's *Rhetoric*. In it, Aristotle writes that 'Empedocles too says the same about not killing any living creature, claiming that this is not right for some people and wrong for others: "But what is lawful for all extends unbroken through the wide-ruling air & measureless sunlight.""[8]

## Social contract theory

Later, the Greek philosopher and historian Plutarch (c. 46–120 CE) wrote several texts on how humans ought to treat nonhuman animals, including *On the Cleverness of Animals*, *On the Eating of Flesh* and *That Beasts are Rational*. Many of his arguments about animals are responses to claims made by Stoic philosophers that animals can be used as humans see fit. In *On Moral Ends*, Cicero writes of the latter:

> But though they hold that there is a code of law which binds humans together, the Stoics do not consider that any such code exists between humans and other animals. Chrysippus made the famous remark that all other things were created for the sake of humans and gods but that humans and gods were created for the sake of their own community and society; and so humans can use animals for their own benefit with impunity.[9]

Stoics such as Chrysippus, who lived in the third century BCE, argued that although nonhuman animals can feel, humans are superior because they have the power of language and reason, and thus the capacity to make and obey laws. The idea that being able to understand and comply with legal and moral laws is

necessary for possessing rights is common. It often
appears in what is known as the social contract
tradition. Social contract theory is the idea that political
communities are bound by rules that constitute
reciprocal contractual agreements between citizens.
The most famous modern example, from 1971, is
found in John Rawls' *A Theory of Justice*, which was
influenced by earlier Enlightenment figures including
Immanuel Kant, Thomas Hobbes and John Locke. Like
Chrysippus, Rawls argues against including nonhuman
animals in principles of justice:

> While I have not maintained that the capacity for a sense
> of justice is necessary in order to be owed the duties
> of justice, it does seem that we are not required to give
> strict justice anyway to creatures lacking this capacity.
> But it does not follow that there are no requirements at
> all in regard to them, nor in our relations with the natural
> order. Certainly it is wrong to be cruel to animals and the
> destruction of a whole species can be a great evil. The
> capacity for feelings of pleasure and pain and for the
> forms of life of which animals are capable clearly imposes
> duties of compassion and humanity in their case.[10]

Later theorists such as Mary Midgley[11] asserted that
Rawls was wrong to exclude nonhuman animals from
justice. Midgley argued that justice ought to be based
on compassion and protecting the vulnerable rather
than capacity for reason. If it is not, then children and
those with severe cognitive impairments will also be
excluded (see Box 3.1).

Back in the first century CE, however, Plutarch took a different route. Rather than denying that we owe duties only to rational beings, he instead tries to show that nonhuman animals are rational in some sense. To do this, he claims that animals can possess many character traits found in humans, such as courage, temperance and honesty. Indeed, animals often possess those qualities to a higher degree than humans. Unfortunately, Plutarch's *On the Eating of Flesh* only survives as a fragment and comes to an end just as he looks as though he might make an argument for something like rights: 'Let us, however, now examine the point whether we really have no compact of justice with animals ...'.

The fact that so much of this early work is lost and fragmentary is very frustrating. However, many of Plutarch's arguments are also repeated by the philosopher Porphyry (*c.* 234–305 CE). Porphyry lived in the city of Tyre, in modern-day Lebanon. Although he was a citizen of the Roman empire, he wrote in Greek and was part of the Pythagorean tradition. In *On Abstinence from Killing Animals*, Porphyry writes a letter to his friend Firmus Castricius. Firmus, a fellow Pythagorean, has let his vegetarianism lapse and so Porphyry writes to try to persuade him back into the fold. Like Plutarch, he attempts to prove the Stoics wrong by arguing that nonhumans possess language and reason, even if not to the same degree as humans. To make this point, Porphyry writes: 'it does not follow, if we have more intelligence than other animals, that on that account they are to be deprived of intelligence;

as neither must it be said, that partridges do not fly, because hawks fly higher ...'.[12]

## Virtue ethics

It would be easy to mistake many of the previous arguments for justification for animal rights. When al-Ma'arrī writes of consuming milk, honey and eggs as constituting theft or Empedocles of laws against killing nonhuman animals that apply to all, these look very much like rights claims. Likewise, descriptions of the suffering of animals in Plutarch or observations about similarities between humans and animals in Porphyry anticipate later arguments in favour of animal rights. Nevertheless, it is probably a mistake to describe any of these thinkers as arguing for rights as we know them. As Myles Burnyeat suggests, the arguments made by Empedocles and others in the same tradition are better thought of as concerning the character a good person ought to cultivate than as about rights and justice.[13]

Ancient Greek ethical thought is part of a tradition we now call virtue ethics. Virtue ethicists say that the focus of ethics should be excellence in moral character: about the kind of person we should be. A virtuous character is one that contributes to human flourishing and happiness. Because ethics, under this account, is essentially inward-looking and personal, it is distinct from rights-based ethical frameworks. Rights are about what we owe to one another and the actions that we are required to do or not do. The foundation of a rights claim is the interest of the rights-holder, not the person who owes a corresponding duty to them. Virtue-based claims reverse the focus of that ethical relationship.

The virtue-based arguments in ancient Greek and Neoplatonist[14] writings are like those found in ancient Chinese texts. In the works of Confucian philosopher Mencius (or Mengzi) (376–289 BCE), we find arguments that humans ought to act kindly towards nonhuman animals. Mencius praises a king for being moved to pity by the look of fear in an animal's eyes, saying, 'The attitude of a virtuous man towards animals is this: once having seen them alive he cannot bear to see them die, and once having heard their cry, he cannot bear to eat their flesh. That is why a virtuous person keeps a distance from his kitchen.'[15] The Confucian tradition urges sensitivity towards nonhuman animals but does so by reference to excellence of human character and it is clear that humans are to be regarded as superior.[16]

Compared with virtue-based accounts, the letters and poems of al-Ma'arrī appear much more hospitable to animal rights arguments. Al-Ma'arrī clearly places the focus of his concern on the interests of nonhuman animals themselves. Nevertheless, his arguments stop short of suggesting that everyone ought to be a vegan. Rather, the kind treatment of animals is portrayed as a morally permissible way of behaving, which he has chosen for himself. There is a strong chance that al-Ma'arrī did not go further because he was trying to avoid putting himself at odds with Islamic doctrine, for which he would probably have been executed.

Nevertheless, his description of the kind treatment of animals as permissible rather than required means that al-Ma'arrī's position is one of benevolence towards animals rather than an animal rights view. The animal rights arguments that we see today only begin to be made in recognizable form in the eighteenth century.

Yet despite the lack of a rights position, the writings of the ancient Greeks influenced later thought. For example, Plutarch's surviving works were widely translated and distributed during the Renaissance. In 1559, the French bishop Jacques Amyot published a translation of Plutarch's *Lives* and in 1572 the *Moralia*. These were read by and proved influential on the French philosopher Michel de Montaigne. In 1580, Montaigne published his famous essay 'On Cruelty'. In it, he observes a link between callousness towards animals and cruelty towards one's fellow human beings. After noting the similarities between humans and other animals, he rejects the idea of a natural right over animals:

> when among the more moderate opinions I meet with arguments that try to show the close resemblance between us and the animals, and how much of a share they have in our greatest privileges, and with how much probability they are likened to us, truly I beat down a lot of our presumption and willingly resign that imaginary kingship that people give us over the other creatures.[17]

Later, in another essay, he writes 'it is apparent that it is not by a true judgment, but by foolish pride and stubbornness, that we set ourselves before the other animals'.[18]

Montaigne wrote at a time when the idea of natural rights was just beginning to be expressed in ways that are familiar and recognizable today. By the mid-seventeenth century there were complex articulations of natural rights in the writings of Thomas Hobbes and Hugo Grotius. In 1776 the American Declaration of Independence was proclaimed, holding it self-evident that 'all men are created equal, that they are endowed by their Creator with certain unalienable Rights, that among these are Life, Liberty and the pursuit of Happiness'. Following the Revolution in 1789 came the French Declaration of the Rights of Man and of the Citizen, which referred to 'the natural, unalienable and sacred rights of man'.

It was only after natural rights for humans began to be described and fought for that philosophers started to make clearly recognizable arguments about animal rights. The best early example of this can be found in the preface to the Swiss philosopher Jean-Jacques Rousseau's 1755 *Discourse on Inequality*:

> an end can also be made to the ancient dispute about the participation of animals in natural law, for it is clear that, lacking intelligence and freedom, they cannot recognise this law; since, however, they share to some extent in our nature by virtue of their having sensations, it will be judged that they must also participate in natural right, and that man is subject to some kind of duties toward them. Indeed, it seems that if I am obligated to do no evil to my

fellow man, it is less because he is a rational being than because he is a sentient being – a property that, because it is common to both animals and men, should at least give the beast the right not to be needlessly mistreated by man.[19]

Here, Rousseau argues that just because nonhuman animals cannot act morally doesn't mean that moral duties are not owed to them. Rousseau's claim is that it is the capacity to suffer rather than reason that underpins rights. Sadly, Rousseau doesn't build on his remarks on nonhuman animals, but the passage remains an important marker in the intellectual history of animal rights.[20]

## Kantian ethics

Several of the thinkers mentioned so far make the argument that we ought to treat nonhuman animals well because doing so makes us more likely to treat other humans better. In *Emile*, Rousseau argues for raising children as vegetarians because 'it is certain that great eaters of meat are in general more cruel and ferocious than other men'.[21] Inspired by Rousseau, Mary Wollstonecraft, writing in 1792, develops a feminist version of this, arguing that children should be educated to be kind to nonhuman animals. Wollstonecraft claims that the behaviour of children, especially boys, towards animals is linked with 'domestic tyranny over wives, children, and servants'.[22] (Contemporary research shows that these writers may have been on to something.)[23]

The most famous example of the argument comes from German philosopher Immanuel Kant.

Kantian ethics is part of a school of moral philosophy known as deontology, from the Greek for duty or obligation. Kant argues that what makes humans worthy of moral consideration is their capacity for rationality. Rationality makes us moral beings, able to choose whether to act upon our desires, and this separates us from other animals. Because we are rational, we are deserving of either praise or blame for the things that we do, and we are able to abide by laws that we have made for ourselves. Kant separates the world into the rational (persons) and the non-rational (things). The core of his philosophy is the injunction that we must never treat persons as if they are things: 'So act that you use the humanity, whether in your own person or in the person of any other, always at the same time as an end, never merely as a means.'[24]

Persons are ends-in-themselves; non-persons are mere instruments for the satisfaction of the ends of persons. Despite thinking that nonhuman animals are things, and thus not worthy of consideration for their own sakes, Kant nevertheless argued for treating them well. He did so because he thought that treating animals badly will make people more likely to treat other humans badly. We have duties to animals, he argues, but these are not for the sake of animals themselves. Our duties to treat them kindly are duties towards wider humanity: 'Our duties towards animals, then, are indirect duties towards mankind.'[25]

Despite arguing against animal rights, Kant's argument is important. One reason for this is because it shows that the idea of animal rights was in the consciousness of philosophers, even if only to require refutation.[26] Beyond this, however, the idea that respecting people requires treating them as ends-in-themselves and never using them merely as a means to an end provides much of the foundation for modern

**Box 2.2: Where are all the women?**

One feature of the intellectual history of animal rights up to this point really stands out: the lack of women. The reason for this is misogyny and patriarchy. Throughout much of history, women have been systematically excluded from political and intellectual life. Women have had fewer opportunities to study, write and be published, and their scholarship has been discounted. Social structures and attitudes have each contributed. This has been a particular problem in philosophy, partly because femininity has been associated with sentimentality and masculinity with rationality, and because women were considered intellectually inferior.[27] Indeed, sexist stereotypes have frequently been used to attack arguments for animal rights by linking them with femininity.[28] Despite their exclusion, women have often led the way in animal protection campaigns and movements, and have made important theoretical contributions to the philosophical debates.

rights-based and contractualist ethical thinking (see later in this chapter). Modern animal rights thinking is often based on the idea that nonhuman animals ought to also be treated as ends-in-themselves.

## Utilitarianism

Towards the end of the eighteenth and in the early nineteenth century, animal rights claims start to appear in many other Western texts, and these coincide with an upsurge in political and civic society campaigning around the treatment of nonhuman animals. One particularly interesting line of thought emerges with the birth of utilitarian philosophy. Utilitarianism is a philosophy that has had a significant positive influence on animal rights while also being hostile to the concept of moral rights. Utilitarianism asserts we should act in ways that maximize good consequences. Utilitarians say that every choice we make should be evaluated in terms of the balance of good over bad that it produces. Good consequences, for utilitarians, are those that produce happiness or pleasure (utility), and bad ones are those that lead to pain and suffering (disutility). When we are trying to decide what to do, the utilitarian argues that we should act in ways that create the maximum possible utility in the world, and that we should do so by counting everyone's utility equally and impartially: everyone's happiness counts the same.

Utilitarianism is an extremely demanding moral theory; it allows only for two categories of action:

those that are required by morality and those that are forbidden. Any act that does not maximize happiness or pleasure is forbidden; acts that do maximize it are required. The reason that this view is generally considered hostile to rights is that considerations like freedom, justice, fairness, promise-keeping and so forth are only thought to matter insofar as they contribute to maximizing utility. If breaking promises, keeping slaves or persecuting minorities are the best way to maximize happiness then utilitarianism says that we are required to do these things and that they are morally good. The purpose of moral rights is to protect individuals, while the goal of utilitarianism is to produce the greatest balance of happiness. Utilitarian arguments against the evils of slavery will say that slavery always, or nearly always, fails to produce the greatest amount of happiness. Similarly, a utilitarian argument for keeping promises will tend to say that a presumption in favour of promise-keeping is the best way to ensure social conditions that maximize happiness.

In 1789, thirty-four years after Rousseau published his *Discourse on Inequality*, the English utilitarian philosopher Jeremy Bentham published *An Introduction to the Principles of Morals and Legislation*, a book that contains perhaps the most famous passage in animal rights history:

> The day may come, when the rest of the animal creation may acquire those rights which never could have been withholden from them but by the hand of tyranny. The French have already discovered that the blackness of

the skin is no reason why a human being should be
abandoned without redress to the caprice of a tormentor.
It may come one day to be recognised, that the number
of the legs, the villosity [hairiness] of the skin, or the
termination of the os sacrum [bone at the spine's base],
are reasons equally insufficient for abandoning a sensitive
being to the same fate. What else is it that should trace the
insuperable line? Is it the faculty of reason, or, perhaps,
the faculty of discourse? But a full-grown horse or dog is
beyond comparison a more rational, as well as a more
conversable animal, than an infant of a day, or a week, or
even a month, old. But suppose the case were otherwise,
what would it avail? the question is not, Can they reason?
nor, Can they talk? but, Can they suffer?[29]

This passage appears in a lengthy footnote to a short discussion of the place of animals in Western legal systems. Bentham notes that a legal distinction taken from Roman law that separates legal entities into persons or things has led to the suffering of animals being ignored: 'Other animals, which on account of their interests having been neglected by the insensibility of the ancient jurists, stand degraded into the class of *things*.'[30] But, Bentham argues, when thinking about how to maximize utility, we ought to include the pleasures and pains felt by nonhuman animals in our calculations. This claim, and the powerful way he expressed it, proved important for several reasons. One was to highlight that the denial of legal rights to nonhuman animals simply on grounds of species membership is arbitrary.

In the 1970s this phenomenon was termed 'speciesism' by the psychologist Richard Ryder. Later that decade, the term was popularized by the utilitarian philosopher Peter Singer in his influential 1975 book *Animal Liberation*. Like Bentham, Singer drew attention to the plight of nonhuman animals by comparing their treatment to forms of human oppression. In doing so, he made his arguments about injustice, and thus about political, rather than merely personal, morality.

Another important element of Bentham's argument is the consideration of animal suffering alongside human suffering. By including animal suffering in the utilitarian calculus, it follows that human pleasures and pains can be outweighed by those of other animals. Later, Singer termed this the 'equal consideration of interests principle'. Finally, Bentham's argument was important because, like Rousseau's, it shifted attention away from rationality as the basis of moral concern and on to sentience.

I've mentioned already that utilitarianism isn't compatible with the idea of moral rights (although it can readily accept legal rights). Indeed, Bentham thought the idea of natural rights dangerous and incoherent, famously referring to them as 'nonsense upon stilts'. Contrary to the idea of natural or moral rights, Bentham thought the term 'law' could only be meaningfully applied to socially created rules. Appeal to natural law undermined the status of democratically agreed laws. Nevertheless, he still favoured legal constraints on the treatment of nonhuman animals, which is a significant part of the purpose of, and argument for, animal rights. Under Bentham's view, governments should create laws that maximize the happiness of their populations rather than protect natural rights. Later thinkers in the utilitarian tradition, like Singer, have also been at pains to distance themselves from rights-based language.[31]

It's worth noting that Bentham's focus was on cruel treatment. He was careful to state that he thought it morally permissible to eat nonhuman animals. This was because he did not think animals have the capacity to anticipate future pains, so they don't lose anything by dying. Additionally, he thought that nonhuman animals suffer more in the wild than they might in agriculture. However, because they can suffer, we must take care how we treat them. This approach is a feature of the utilitarian framework. Killing and causing pain are justified if they maximize happiness.

Although it is ironic that the utilitarian tradition has had a powerful positive impact on arguments for animal rights, it is also understandable. As we shall see, grounding moral concern in sentience and interests rather than rationality, and rejecting arbitrary species distinctions, are considerations that go beyond utilitarianism. Similarly, the use of overtly political terms such as tyranny and liberation connects concern for nonhumans with political struggle and the concept of justice in ways that need not be tied to a particular moral philosophy.

During the nineteenth century, concerns about the cruelty of vivisection and the growth of animal welfare movements prompted several other philosophers to make their own contributions. In 1819 Arthur Schopenhauer wrote in *The World as Will and Representation* that humanity does not have a right to perform vivisection on higher animals,[32] and Schopenhauer, whose thinking was influenced by Buddhism and Hinduism, justified his claim on the capacity of nonhuman animals to suffer. In *On the Basis of Morality* Schopenhauer attacked Kant for categorizing nonhuman animals as mere things and laid into any system of morality that denied rights to animals because they lack rationality.[33] He didn't mince his words: 'I regard such propositions as revolting & abominable … shame on such a morality.'[34] And, in his essay 'On religion' he had this to say of a scientist who conducted an experiment to measure the effects of starvation on brain chemistry by starving two rabbits to death:

> Do these gentlemen of the scalpel and crucible even consider in their wildest dreams that they are human beings first and chemists afterwards? – How can one sleep peacefully while animals suckled by their mothers are kept under lock and key to suffer the agonizing and slow death of starvation?[35]

Irish suffragist Frances Power Cobbe was also concerned about vivisection and authored one of the earliest texts devoted entirely to the subject of animal rights. In an 1863 article published in *Fraser's Magazine*, 'The Rights of Man and the Claims of Brutes', Cobbe argued that the capacity for sentience creates an absolute duty not to cause pointless suffering:

**Figure 2.2: Frances Power Cobbe**

Frances Power Cobbe (1822–1904) was a journalist, philosopher, Conservative unionist politician and campaigner, who fought for women's suffrage and animal rights. Cobbe played a key role in enacting the Cruelty to Animals Act 1876.

> The highest end of a merely sentient being is enjoyment of pleasure and freedom from pain, i.e., happiness; ... we are bound to seek the sentient being's happiness because he is capable of happiness, ... We may take animal life (that is, the whole sum of the animal's pleasures) for the interests of science; but we must take it with no needless infliction of pain.[36]

Because Cobbe mistakenly thought that eating meat was necessary to live, she stopped short of specifying that nonhuman animals have a right against being killed. Nevertheless, to kill an animal required demonstrating a clear benefit and suffering had to be minimized. Her early position was very close to what American philosopher Robert Nozick later described as 'utilitarianism for animals, Kantianism for people'.[37] Later, Cobbe developed a more rights-based approach, rejecting utilitarianism and forbidding the infliction of suffering not intended to benefit the animal itself.[38]

## Box 2.3: Animal rights and women's suffrage

### Figure 2.3: Anti-vivisection campaigners, 1903

Animal protection movements have often been led by women. Early anti-vivisection campaigns were often connected with women's suffrage and women-led peace and temperance campaigns.

Frances Cobbe wrote during a period in which Western women had begun to vigorously assert their rights. These campaigns made it more difficult for men to marginalize women's intellectual writings. As a result, we also start to see more texts written by women about animal rights and animal protection. Indeed, there is a strong connection between feminist and vegetarian movements during the nineteenth century, and between campaigns for animal protection, women's suffrage, and the peace and temperance movements. Carol Adams details how the early leaders of the Women's Christian Temperance Movement in the US were vegetarians, and that when the World Temperance Movement met in London in 1895 they began with a vegetarian reception, organized by the Women's Vegetarian Union. Women's rights activists such as Anna Kingsford, Harriet Beecher Stowe, Frances Willard, Annie Besant and Frances Power Cobbe were also prominent anti-vivisection campaigners.[39]

The end of the century saw the publication of a number of works by Henry Salt, a prolific English writer, academic and social reformer. His first book, *A Plea for Vegetarianism*, appeared in 1886 and was described by his friend Mahatma Gandhi as having been influential in cementing his commitment to vegetarianism.[40] In 1892 Salt published *Animals' Rights: Considered in Relation to Social Progress*, followed by an essay 'The Rights of Animals' in the *International Journal of Ethics*. Salt, with some exaggeration, claimed this as 'the first academic essay to address animal ethics'. Nevertheless, these texts are notable for their clear, sustained arguments for animal rights. *Animals' Rights: Considered in Relation to Social Progress* begins: 'Have the lower animals rights? Undoubtedly, if men have.' It goes on to make a sentience-based argument containing many of the elements seen in contemporary works on animal rights. Salt's book is often considered one of the most important texts in the history of animal rights.

By now, the idea of animal rights had been firmly cemented in philosophical thought. Nevertheless, it was not until the 1970s that it began to really take off as the basis for political campaigning. In the intervening period, two world wars slowed progress until a growing concern with environmental issues, catalyzed in 1962 by the publication of Rachel Carson's *Silent Spring*, also began to reinvigorate the animal protection movement. In 1964 Ruth Harrison's influential book *Animal Machines* sparked public debate around the wrongs of intensive animal agriculture. In response, the UK government published the Bramble report, which recommended introducing laws to protect the welfare of farmed animals. This report marked the first time a government had explicitly used the concept of sentience to justify welfare legislation. Despite these advances, much of the debate until the 1970s focused on improving welfare rather than protecting rights.

In the 1970s, more developed positions on animal rights helped inspire the modern animal rights movement. The intellectual efforts of various philosophers assisted in creating a clear distinction between those fighting to gradually improve animal welfare and those looking to codify moral rights in law. This distinction between welfarist and liberationist or abolitionist positions persists today (more on this in Chapter 6). In the UK, a group of thinkers known as the Oxford Group, because they grew out of Oxford University friendship circles, produced a series of academic texts and engaged in public philosophy around animal rights. One of the earliest examples was Ros Godlovitch's article 'Animals and Morals', published in 1971 in *Philosophy*, the journal of the Royal Institute of Philosophy. This article, together with a book co-edited by Godlovitch shortly afterwards, precipitated a wave of animal rights texts.

Of these, Singer's *Animal Liberation* (referred to previously) was very widely read by animal activists and has been spoken of by many as having inspired them to action. Singer's book helped to give birth to the modern movement and turn animal rights into a political ideology. A debate between Singer and American philosopher Tom Regan, conducted in a series of academic texts, assisted in cementing the distinction between utilitarian and deontological positions on nonhuman animals.

# 3
# RIGHTS, INTERESTS AND CHOICES

The intellectual history of animal rights has introduced us to some important philosophical positions, such as the idea that animals matter for their own sakes and that rights represent enforceable moral rules. But, as we saw from examples like Kant, there are people who think that only human beings can have rights. In this section, I want to illustrate how animal rights theorists often respond to this claim, and then to show how sentience acts as a justification for animal rights.

One important way that theorists try to demonstrate that nonhuman animals have rights is known as the argument from awkward cases.[1]

This form of argument is based on assumptions about what makes a good moral theory, which include that it should be consistent, coherent and rational. If moral principles change even where circumstances

**Box 3.1: Awkward cases**

Arguments that justify human superiority by reference to the capacity for reason are vulnerable to the argument from awkward cases. Simply put, at some point in our lives, all of us will lack reason, moral agency and the power of language. Indeed, many animals possess higher cognitive capacities than many humans. Next to humans, dolphins are the smartest of the animals. They have complex social structures, communicate in sophisticated ways, use tools, play, engage in cross-species cooperation and are self-aware. Although cross-species intelligence measurement is fraught with problems, it is sometimes said that dolphins are roughly equivalent in intelligence to an average five-to-seven-year-old human. If young children are owed rights despite their lack of reason, then why not dolphins, chimpanzees, elephants and other cognitively sophisticated animals? One possibility is that potential for rationality is what matters, but this argument is pretty weak. We don't tend to think that the reason to protect the interests of children is because they will one day be adults. Nor do we think those children who because of some impairment will never go on to become rational, or those adults who permanently lose the power to reason, should be excluded from having rights.

are the same, if they contradict one another, or if they are arbitrary and lacking justification, then they cannot reliably guide how we act and so aren't much use to us. The argument from awkward cases begins by asking what it is that justifies rights. Usually, the answer is either 'humanity' or some capability such as language, high intelligence, reason or moral agency. Justifying rights on grounds merely of species membership (humanity) appears arbitrary, so it fails as a moral argument. Hence, the claim that denying rights to nonhuman animals is speciesist. But if rights are justified on grounds of capability then a new problem arises. Simply put, there are no capabilities relevant to the possession of rights held by all humans and no nonhuman animals.

That means that, if our justification for rights is to avoid being arbitrary, it must be based on a characteristic that all, or nearly all, humans possess. The most likely characteristic is sentience. In other words, in order to be both consistent and non-arbitrary, we face a choice. If we exclude nonhuman animals from holding rights because of their inability to reason, then we will also have to deny rights to many humans – the awkward cases. If we think all humans ought to have rights, then the only capabilities that will justify this are also likely to be found in nonhumans. Some theorists do indeed opt to exclude the human awkward cases from holding rights, but most of us are likely to consider such a route extremely unpalatable. The more attractive moral principle is to achieve consistency by grounding rights in sentience rather than rationality. Let us now look at how sentience justifies rights in more detail.

The possession of sentience means that nonhuman animals have lives that can get better or worse, and in ways that matter to them. In other words, sentient beings have interests, and they have preferences about those interests. The capacity to experience feelings like pain and pleasure sets sentient beings apart from non-sentient life-forms. Life-forms that lack sentience, like plants, can be harmed, but they lack any subjective experience of those harms. When a branch is broken from a tree, it's bad for the tree, but the tree doesn't have any conscious awareness of the harm. Trees can be harmed, but they do not feel pain and cannot suffer. It is the personal, subjective experience of their lives that provides us with strong reasons to care about nonhuman animals for their own sakes.

The fact that nonhuman animals are sentient ought to influence how we think about them and how we treat them. Indeed, many people think that possessing sentience is enough to justify rights. When people talk about animal rights, they mean that there are strong moral reasons to constrain how people act towards nonhuman animals. As described earlier, rights are special entitlements to something or protections from being treated a certain way. For example, a right against being killed forbids others from killing the right-holder, and a right to be helped requires others to lend assistance. When we say that someone has a moral right to something, we are saying that there ought to be a law to that effect and that denial of the right is wrong, regardless of what the law currently says.

Certain interests generate duties in other people, duties which promote the interests of the right-holder. Not every sort of interest counts for this. The strongest contenders are those interests that prevent us from having any sort of decent life if they aren't met. We can call these basic, vital or non-contingent interests, interests like food and water, bodily security, continued existence and freedom from suffering. These are the interests that our welfare depends on. Rights protect the welfare of individuals by imposing duties on others.[2] Non-contingent interests are different from things that I merely have a present desire or preference for. While writing, I might feel the desire to eat some chocolate. Because eating chocolate will make me happy, I have an interest in having some chocolate. However, nobody is under a duty to provide me with chocolate because of this. I can live without chocolate. Under this theory, rights serve to identify the interests that are sufficiently important as to impose duties on others and that should therefore be protected by law.[3]

The biggest competitor to the interest (or benefit) theory of rights is known as the will (or choice) theory. The will theory holds that the purpose of rights is to protect choices rather than interests. To have a right, under this theory, is to be able to control the fulfilment of the duty correlated with it. If I have a right to some of your money because you owe me a debt, then you have a duty to pay me that money. But I can choose to forgo my right, absolving you of your debt. Or I can transfer the debt to someone else. I may also choose to enforce the debt if you refuse to repay me. The will theory says that this power to choose how duties are fulfilled is what defines and justifies rights. A consequence of this is that beings unable to make choices cannot be rights-holders. The will theory thus excludes infants, nonhuman animals and those with severe cognitive impairments from being rights-holders. Partly because of this, and because it is not easily compatible with existing legal frameworks, the will theory is a minority view.

Under the interest theory, the rights that an individual possesses relate to the interests they have. For example, women's sex-based rights relate to interests they possess but men do not, such as in maternity care. Similarly, most adults have an interest in autonomy that children lack, and so forth. In terms of animal rights, the most common rights claims are based on the interest against suffering and the interest in continued existence (life). Every sentient being has a strong interest in not suffering or experiencing pain; and every being with preferences and an identity that persists over time has an interest in not being killed. To kill a being with memories and future-directed desires robs them of the potential for realizing future goods. At the same time, the interest theory excludes beings from possessing rights where they lack an interest. Thus, beings with the ability to make choices, and to make and revise long-term plans – a category that excludes most, if not all, nonhumans – have an interest in having their autonomy protected. Beings that lack these capacities do not have an interest in exercising autonomy and thus lack rights connected with it.

While rights against being killed or made to suffer are the most obvious and most commonly argued-for rights animals might be owed, they are far from the only ones. For instance, the animals we domesticate for farming purposes are extremely social. If they weren't social, we couldn't confine tens of thousands of them in close quarters.

## Box 3.2: Animal personalities

Animals such as cows have complex mental lives and individual personalities, and they form relationships that matter a great deal to them. Cows form enduring friendships, they choose grooming and grazing partners, and mothers and calves form lasting bonds. Scientific evidence has shown increases in stress hormones when they are separated from their herd members, or crowded, or placed with unfamiliar cows – all common farming practices. When a cow is distressed, herd-mates carry out consoling behaviour by gently touching and licking, and they grieve the losses of loved ones. Other research has shown similar capabilities in other farmed animals. Pigs, for example, are highly intelligent and inquisitive animals, possessing long memories and experiencing emotions like fear, happiness, pain and excitement. They enjoy playing, and become bored and depressed when unable to spend time with other pigs that they like. Loneliness manifests in illness and negative behavioural symptoms. Pigs even show evidence of preparing and planning for the future. In pigs, cows, sheep and chickens, research has shown that individual differences in animals can be seen in distinct personalities and preferences.

Without good-quality relationships, social animals cannot flourish. Indeed, one of the reasons we know so much about the negative impacts of loneliness and isolation on humans is because of deprivation experiments performed on social nonhuman animals (more on this in Chapter 4). All of this suggests that social animals have a strong interest in being able to enjoy good relationships, and perhaps therefore relationship rights. These rights have the same justification for them as the human rights to a family relationship and association. If nonhuman animals have rights to good relationships, then farming practices that control, disrupt and destroy their relationships will seriously wrong them.[4]

Similarly, some animals can live good lives only in particular habitats. For example, there is evidence that primates suffer a loss of wellbeing when their living conditions do not resemble their natural habitats. In the wild, populations of orangutans in different locations develop different cultural practices, and they spend their days roaming extensively in their territories. As a result, zookeepers need to expend a great deal of effort to prevent orangutans in zoos from becoming bored and depressed. Other animals need the ecological conditions in particular habitats to survive. Cases like these suggest that for at least some animals there is a strong interest in being able to live in their natural habitats, generating rights to live there and have them protected from destruction.[5]

## Justice and political morality

Rights are empty if unenforced. This is where the concept of justice comes in, which takes us into the realm of social and political morality. Justice describes what is morally owed to individuals. Principles of justice set out what each of us can rightfully demand of one another, such as equal treatment or freedom from enslavement. If I am owed something as a matter of justice, then I am wronged if it is not provided to me. Principles of justice don't cover everything that matters morally, merely the universally required minimums. If I am owed nothing else, I am at least owed justice. Justice relates to rights because the area of morality it describes is enforceable. Rights serve as a way of describing and implementing principles of justice. For example, principles of justice might require that no one is enslaved, assaulted, killed or tormented, and these principles can then be embodied in rights against enslavement, assault, killing and torture.

One very important question about justice and rights is: who gets to enforce them? Who has the authority to determine when a right has been violated and what should be done about it? These are perennial questions of political philosophy, concerning power, legitimacy and the use of force. They are why issues of rights and justice are matters of political rather than personal morality. One of the key goals of political philosophy is to set out the conditions under which a state can act in a just manner, so that its exercise of authority can be regarded as legitimate. Animal rights theorists argue that our political communities will remain unjust so long as the rights of nonhuman animals continue to be violated in serious and systematic ways.

Animal rights represent interests that are so important that frustrating them without very good cause (such as self-defence) ought to be forbidden – in other words, a way of marking concern for animals as a matter of justice rather than preference. Those who reject animal rights say that our treatment of other animals ought to be a matter of personal choice even if they think things like cruelty are wrong. One of the key tasks of animal rights theorists is to identify the interests that should be protected with rights, and therefore where force may be permitted to ensure people comply with the demands of justice.

Another interesting question about justice concerns what we call special, acquired or associative duties. Some theorists argue that justice is something that is owed primarily to members of one's own political community. We owe these duties, so it is argued, because a political community, such as a state, is a cooperative scheme between free and equal citizens for mutual advantage.[6] Certain benefits can only be obtained when we work together, at some cost to ourselves. As a result, everyone involved in that scheme – every member of the community – owes something to the other members of the scheme. Cooperating in this way generates special rights (such as political rights to representation), and duties (such as the duty not to free-ride on the efforts of others in the scheme).

This is a version of the social contract model of justice mentioned in Chapter 2. Generally, this model starts by assuming a set of basic rights and then adding additional ones that arise from being part of the association (such as political rights). People outside the community might still be owed basic rights, but they can expect less than those within it. Other rights might be possessed by non-members based on historical debts and agreements. For example, a community that wrongfully harmed another might gain obligations to make reparations, thus giving members of the harmed community rights against them. In terms of animal rights, this model requires us to ask whether some nonhuman animals might be considered members of a political community and what that means in terms of their rights. It also prompts us to think about how those animals outside the community should be treated. We will return to these questions towards the end of Chapter 5.

If we look back at the intellectual history of animal rights, we can identify a preoccupation with what we call negative rights. Negative rights are rights not to be treated in certain ways; they are rights of non-interference. These include rights against being killed, being made to suffer, being held captive, and all the other possible rights we've so far described. However, more recently, theorists have also argued for *positive* rights. These describe entitlements to certain goods or treatment. Examples of positive rights include the right to a minimum standard of living and the right to assistance when in dire need. In Chapter 5, we will see what granting both positive and negative rights for animals and including them within the scope of justice might mean in practice. Before that, let us explore the consequences of granting animals rights in familiar cases.

# 4

# CASE STUDIES: ANIMALS IN THE FARM, HOME, ZOO AND LAB

Imagine for a moment that nonhuman animals have been granted the same moral rights as humans. What might society look like if we tried to implement those rights by protecting them in law? It would be very different indeed. So different in fact that you might be struggling to picture it. In case that's true, in this chapter I explore how four common ways we interact with animals, either directly or indirectly, would change: in farming, as companion animals, in zoos and in scientific research. Providing some detail on the impact animal rights would have on these four cases can make imagining justice for nonhuman animals seem less abstract. This work will lead on to discussion in Chapter 5 of some emerging and longstanding issues for animal rights. Engaging with topics like wild animal suffering, new research on animal minds and the idea of nonhuman animals as citizens helps to illustrate the limits of animal rights theory and the sorts of problems that must be overcome.

## Animal agriculture

If we take farming first, we know already that the animal rights position rules out causing nonhuman animals to suffer for the sake of human interests. We also know that most farmed animals are kept in factory farms. Factory farms are places where nonhuman animals are intensively farmed: animals are bred and raised in cramped conditions, using methods designed to make production as efficient and predictable as possible. Often, factory-farmed animals spend their entire lives indoors, without any natural light, and with every part of their lives carefully controlled. Factory farming is intended to minimize costs and maximize production, with animals bred and raised to grow very quickly to a large size, and produce great quantities of milk, eggs or flesh. That means that most farmed animals live and die in confined spaces, unable to carry out their natural activities, enjoy freedom and flourish. The Sentience Institute has estimated that more than 90 per cent globally of all farmed animals are factory farmed. This figure includes nearly all farmed fish, which make up around 78 per cent of factory farmed animals. Meanwhile, 74 per cent of farmed land animals are estimated to be factory farmed, with the most numerous of these being chickens.[1] The Food and Agriculture Organization (FAO) of the United

Nations estimates that globally more than seventy billion chickens are slaughtered each year. Numerically, the estimate for 2020 looks like this: 70,767,577,000. Exact figures are difficult to find for the world,[2] but in the US the percentage of chickens that are factory farmed is around 99.9 per cent.

The high-density housing of these animals means that they frequently suffer injury and ill health, with high risks from disease outbreaks. For example, in the UK, where welfare standards are relatively high, a factory-farmed chicken will live in flocks of over forty thousand birds, with roughly 19 adult birds housed per square

**Figure 4.1: The face of a pig on its way to slaughter**

Despite being highly intelligent creatures, pigs are the third most slaughtered animals in the world. Roughly 1.5 billion pigs are killed for food each year, a figure that continues to rise dramatically.

metre. In 2021 one Russian chicken plant (it's hard to describe it as a farm) suffered an outbreak of avian flu. After 101,000 birds died from the disease, the rest of the flock of 924,612 chickens were slaughtered to prevent it spreading further.[3]

A combination of selective breeding, genetic manipulation, and careful control of food and environmental conditions means that chickens typically reach the desired weight and are slaughtered at just five to six weeks old. Rapid growth and significant rapid weight gain lead to serious health complications, with heart attacks and lameness common. Chickens also frequently suffer chemical burns from lying in their own faeces, which are high in ammonia. To prevent them feather-pecking due to boredom and overcrowding, chickens have their beaks painfully trimmed. This is the reality of modern farming.

If rights against suffering and being killed were recognized, none of this would be permitted. Factory farming would be outlawed. Might that leave room for other forms of non-intensive animal agriculture? Perhaps. Animal rights need not imply veganism, but they do imply something close to it. Animals able to live good lives, to realize their most important preferences and have their interests satisfied might still be farmed. It's easy to imagine that a free-roaming chicken could live a good life, with its rights respected, while still having some of its eggs collected. Similarly, some breeds of sheep can shed their wool without the need for distressing shearing practices. The continued production of dairy products seems unlikely, since this industry depends on repeated cycles of forced impregnation and then separation of mother and child (with unwanted children subsequently killed). And perhaps meat and leather might sometimes be available from animals that had died of natural causes. But it's very difficult to see how animal agriculture could survive as an industry.

It's common to hear several sorts of responses to the scenario above. One is to express the worry that animal rights would see a huge reduction in animal populations, perhaps including the extinction of some species. From an animal rights perspective, such a concern is not especially troubling. This is because rights are focused on protecting the entitlements of individual animals. In that respect, the continuation of a species only matters insofar as it contributes to the wellbeing of individuals. Some ethical frameworks, such as ecocentric versions of environmental ethics, argue that collectives or systems, including species, populations or ecosystems, have value that can be separated from the individual beings that make them up. As a result, this kind of thinking allows individuals to be sacrificed for the sake of the collective, putting it at odds with rights-based ethical frameworks. Other, more traditional stewardship conservation approaches regard the loss of a species as bad in large part because it represents lost opportunities for humans to enjoy it. Again, the animal rights view rejects this kind of anthropocentric thinking.

Another response is to claim that ending animal agriculture somehow harms nonhuman animals because it robs future animals of the benefit of living. Perhaps, if they were to live well, it is true that ending animal agriculture would deny some future animals the chance of life and happiness. However, it doesn't make sense to argue that we cause harms to as-yet-non-existent animals by failing to cause them to exist.

The connected response is to argue that so long as animals are given a good life by a farmer, killing them is permissible. Indeed, it is sometimes claimed that the farming relationship represents a sort of contract or exchange: the farmer provides the animal with a good life and in return the animal owes the farmer their life and their body. But, while it is true that some ways of farming might allow for animals to live contented lives, it doesn't follow that this generates a permission to kill them. Bringing a being into existence doesn't grant a right to kill it. However a being came into existence, once it can feel and thus has preference-based interests, the rights position rules out killing it.

Does all this mean that, under a rights view, meat is off the table? Not necessarily. It might still be possible to produce meat, at quantity, in ways that do not violate rights. For example, a great deal of effort is currently being expended to grow meat and other animal products in laboratories and to industrialize this process. These lab-grown animal products often need a small quantity of animal stem cells to begin the process, but nothing in the cell-harvesting procedure requires serious harm or discomfort to the donor. Another possible way to produce animal products might be to restrict them to species that supposedly lack sentience. For example, it used to be thought by many that fish lacked sentience. However, we now know that this view was mistaken (see Box 5.1, in the next chapter). The conclusions of scientific research are extremely important for animal rights because fish are harvested from the oceans in such vast quantities that their deaths are measured in tonnes rather than by numbers of individual animals. In place of fish, perhaps other classes of creatures might be farmed without risk of rights violations? In this respect, some consider insect farming as the next frontier. Insect farms which produce animal feed are already common, but many companies are trying to expand production and create markets aimed at humans (more on insects in Chapter 5).

As we can see, an animal rights position requires a large shift towards plant-based diets and a great reduction in the use of animal products. However, it doesn't completely rule out the possibility of continued use and consumption in the limited scenarios outlined earlier. Since most agricultural land is currently given over to growing animal feed, such a shift would require less land use and be significantly more environmentally friendly.

## Companion animals

In 1993 British filmmaker and screenwriter Duncan Gibbins suffered third-degree burns while trying to save his cat Elsa from a wildfire in California. Elsa survived, but Gibbins died in hospital from his injuries. In 2022 an Aberdeen man drowned trying to rescue his dog after the latter was frightened by fireworks and fell into the sea. Cases of people taking serious risks to save their companion animals from danger are common, and in 2021 a survey of American dog owners reported that 72 per cent would willingly risk their lives to save their pet. Many people think of their companion animals as close friends or family members, and it's not unusual to hear pet owners claim to love them more than their spouses. Pet owners often love and care for their animals deeply and make considerable sacrifices for their sakes.

Despite the love that many people feel for their companion animals and despite being more strongly protected than animals used in farming and research, these animals remain extremely vulnerable. At some point in their career, most veterinarians will receive a request to have a healthy companion animal killed for trivial reasons. These reasons include things like the purchase of new furniture, the shedding of fur or rehoming a now unwanted pet being too much effort. The problem is widespread enough that the veterinary profession has coined the term 'convenience euthanasia', and their industry magazines contain numerous articles from vets struggling with how best to respond. While most vets will refuse such requests, they are not obliged to. In some cases, vets will accede to the request out of concern that the animal's owner will otherwise attempt to kill the pet themselves, causing serious suffering.

What this shows is that love and concern are not enough to secure animal interests. Their status as property contributes to some people regarding pets merely as a means of satisfying their own ends. If the way we treat nonhuman animals is left up to personal preference, then their most important interests inevitably risk being violated for the most trivial of human interests. The legal status of a companion animal as property means that their owners have the power to decide, for entirely selfish reasons, whether they live or die. The purpose of rights is to prevent such occurrences.

Animal rights theorists are divided on how to address the property status of nonhuman animals. Some theorists argue that animals will never properly be morally respected so long as they can be owned.[4] Part of the reason ownership is problematic is because it conveys something about the nature of the owned thing's value. Property is regarded as valuable for the sake of its owners. The property I own is valuable because it advances my interests (I find it useful, or it makes me happy). In other words, my property is instrumentally valuable to me, it serves as a means to secure my ends. When we assert that it is wrong to own a person, we are often making a Kantian sort of claim that it is wrong to treat others merely as a means (see Chapter 2). If something cannot be owned, it serves as a way of signalling that it has a value beyond its usefulness.

Another way ownership of nonhumans is problematic is that property ownership grants the owner powers to use their property in certain ways without interference. Those powers usually include a right to damage or destroy one's property. For example, selective breeding and practices like ear-cropping of dogs are often carried out for aesthetic reasons and result in serious welfare issues for companion animals.

To avoid nonhumans being regarded as instrumentally valuable, and to reduce the risk of them being harmed, some theorists argue that owning nonhuman animals is wrong. So, one route to protecting nonhuman animals would be to change the law so that nonhuman animals have legal standing, with rights against being owned. If nonhuman animals have such a right, then human–companion animal relationships will need to be radically reconfigured. In practice, this might require the law to recognize such relationships as much more like a perpetual child–parent or foster-carer relationship, with far stronger rights for nonhumans and more stringent duties for human carers and the state.

An alternative position is to accept that nonhuman animals may be property but to change the nature of animal ownership rights. An ownership right actually refers to several powers: to transfer ownership, to use without interference, and to deny others use of property. This bundle of what are called 'incidences of ownership' in legal theory can be configured in different ways for different kinds of property. For example, owners of historically or artistically important buildings in many parts of the world are constrained in what they can do to those buildings: their usage rights are limited. In fact, many legal systems have similar sorts of constraints on what can be done to companion animals. For example, ear-cropping of dogs is illegal in England and Wales, and in Turkey it is illegal to abandon a companion animal where it will be unable to care for itself in a natural way. Owners are often forbidden from killing companion animals themselves and have duties to care for them in certain ways. Thus, it might be possible to strengthen the legal rights of animals in ways that respect their moral rights while also allowing them to be owned and traded.

Why shouldn't defenders of animal rights regard owning animals as straight-up morally objectionable in the same way that we think slavery is wrong? The answer relates to the value and importance of rationality. If a being can reason, then it can make choices. Not only does this make a person capable of acting morally, but it also means that they can make and revise long-term life plans. These capacities are important to the beings that have them, and they are also usually taken to be the defining features of those beings. As a result, rational beings have a strong interest in protecting and nurturing their capacities to evaluate and act upon reasons. So, rational beings have freedom- or autonomy-based rights, such as freedoms to choose and to act according to their conscience, political rights, rights of association, freedom from arbitrary arrest, rights to education and so on. This means that great evils like slavery aren't wrong just because they reduce the welfare of slaves, they are also wrong because the violate the freedom of those enslaved. As the political theorist Isaiah Berlin once remarked, 'A man struggling against his chains or a people against enslavement need not consciously aim at any definite further state. A man need not know how he will use his freedom; he just wants to remove the yoke.'[5]

In other words, for people capable of acting autonomously, freedom may be valuable for its own sake and not just because it enables them to pursue certain goals. Knowing that we are unable to act autonomously because we are subject to the arbitrary will of another can be harmful to us. By the same token, beings that lack rationality don't have any interest in rights to protect rationality. The freedom a cat enjoys by being able to come and go as she pleases is valuable because it directly contributes to her happiness, whereas the freedom a rational being has is also intrinsically valuable. Limiting a cat's freedom only harms her if it makes her unhappy, whereas limiting a person's freedom is wrong in additional ways.

Furthermore, simply knowing that they are someone's property is enough to cause a person serious upset, whereas a creature like a cat lacks this awareness. This means that so long as a companion animal enjoys a high level of welfare, its status as property need not wrong it in the way slavery wrongs a person.[6] Nevertheless, despite the possibility of ownership being compatible with respecting animal rights, it may be, as mentioned previously, that it signifies the wrong way of valuing nonhuman life (see also Chapter 7).

## Zoos

In the 1970s seven elephant calves were captured, probably in Thailand, and shipped to the United States, where they were sold to zoos and circuses. Two of them, named Happy and Grumpy, went to the Bronx Zoo in New York. This pair lived together for 25 years before zookeepers moved them into an enclosure with two unfamiliar elephants. When those elephants charged, Grumpy fell, injuring herself. She never recovered and was later euthanized by staff. Happy was paired with a different companion, who went on to suffer kidney failure and was euthanized four years later. Happy has lived alone since that day in 2006. She spends her days going between a small 1.15-acre rotating exhibit space and an indoor space lined with elephant cages. In the wild, elephants are deeply social creatures, living and roaming in family groups. Female elephants stay with their friends and relatives for their whole lives. Happy's life has been a lonely and unhappy one.

Elephants are extremely intelligent creatures with complex emotions, identities that persist over time and a sense of self. One way that scientists measure the mental complexity of nonhuman animals is through what is known as the mirror self-recognition test (mirror test, for short). Elephants pass the mirror test and so we know that they have a sense of self. Indeed, Happy was the first elephant to do so. We also know that elephants are social and caring, carry out altruistic acts,[7] grieve and show compassion when others are mourning.[8]

**Box 4.1: The mirror test**

The mirror test is used in the study of animal cognition to determine if an animal has a sense of self. Most animals, humans included, react to their first encounter with a mirror as if seeing another creature in it. Some, however, eventually come to recognize that they are seeing themselves. The mirror test involves marking an animal's body and then placing a mirror in front of them. If the animal touches the mark more often when they can see it a mirror, that suggests they know they are looking at themselves. To date, all the great apes together with Asian elephants, bottlenose dolphins, magpies and perhaps even fish, have passed the test.[9]

While Happy's keepers have claimed that she is contented and has her need for companionship satisfied by her bonds with the humans around her, others are not convinced. In 2018 the Nonhuman Rights Project (NhRP) sued the zoo, claiming that Happy ought to be granted the same protections against being held captive as a human. Sadly, in June 2022 New York's highest court ruled by majority against NhRP, concluding that although Happy deserves to be treated with care and compassion, she does not count as a person in law and therefore is not protected by habeas corpus rules against confinement.[10]

Unlike the definition of personhood given in the previous section, legal personhood is not grounded in a particular capacity. Rather, the concept simply refers to whichever entities may possess legal rights on their own behalf. Legal personhood is granted to all humans and, in some legal systems such as those of the US and the UK, to corporations. Elsewhere, natural entities such as rivers and mountains have been granted legal personhood, with state advocates tasked with representing their interests in court.

The NhRP has brought several of these cases, acting on behalf of both elephants and great apes. As is usual in them, judges in the Happy case displayed an unwillingness to allow legal challenges to be used to change the political status quo. Their decision was based on a concern that were they to have accepted the NhRP's argument, then it 'would have an enormous destabilizing impact on modern society' and 'would call into question the very premises underlying pet ownership, the use of service animals, and the enlistment of animals in other forms of work'. Rather than rule on whether Happy ought to be regarded as a person, the court simply refused to consider the arguments. In effect, their ruling expressed the view that the legal status of nonhuman animals ought to be decided outside of the courts, as a matter of politics, not law.

Interestingly, one of the two judges who wrote a minority report on the case, Judge Rowan Wilson, made the point that 'Historically, the Great Writ of habeas corpus was used to challenge detentions that violated no statutory right and were otherwise legal but, in a given case, *unjust*' (my emphasis). By expressing the view that keeping Happy captive is unjust, either because it violates her freedom or because it negatively affects her wellbeing, Wilson was saying that Happy ought to have a right against such treatment. And not just any right – a moral right, because Happy's captivity wrongs her directly. By failing to protect her, the law falls below the standard required by justice and should therefore be changed.

The ruling judge was correct to say that recognizing Happy as a legal person would have profound social implications, but her implication that courts ought to stay neutral on matters of justice is far less obviously true. What we can say is that were animal rights recognized in law, just as in the case of companion

**Figure 4.2: Zoo elephant, 1923**

Animal rights campaigners, such as those in the Nonhuman Rights Project, have argued that imprisonment is bad for some nonhuman animals in much the same way as it is for humans. Being kept captive in a zoo might prevent species such as elephants and higher apes from flourishing. The Nonhuman Rights Project has fought for zoo animal freedoms by attempting to bring legal writs of habeas corpus on behalf of nonhuman animals.

animals, their captivity could only be justified if it could be shown that it did not harm them. For larger animals, particularly those that like to roam widely, it is hard to see how captivity could be permitted.

The presence in zoos of animals with complex mental lives, and with natural behaviours that are hard to permit or substitute in a zoo setting, helps us to think about animal welfare. Animal welfare is a surprisingly complex and debated topic, both in science (how should it be measured, what factors influence it?) and philosophically (what is it?). For example, there are debates about whether welfare relates to how well an animal can engage in natural behaviour for its species; whether it is connected simply to the balance of pleasure experienced over pain; if it is about the satisfaction of preferences, about maintaining a healthy body, or if it describes animal's ability to cope with its environment. At heart, however, welfare describes what is good for an animal for its own sake. In other words, what is non-instrumentally good for it. For sentient beings, what is good for them is a mix of both physical and mental factors. For animals of some species, happiness and preference satisfaction are only possible when they are able to engage in natural activities; in others, it is more connected with bodily comfort. In the case of animals like Happy, wellbeing is being sacrificed for the enjoyment of visitors to the zoo, and for the zoo's economic benefit. While these things might count as morally good, because they advance human interests, they would not count as sufficient reason to trump the rights-claim of a nonhuman animal.

The existence of zoos provides a good illustration of the difference between rights-based approaches to ethics and other ways of valuing animals. For example, zoos are often justified on conservation grounds. They participate in captive breeding programmes, with the aims either of later releasing animals into the wild to bolster free-ranging populations or of preserving species close to extinction. Sometimes, perhaps often, this may mean sacrificing the good of an individual animal for the sake of preserving a species. As we saw in the previous section on animal agriculture , this is not easily justified from a rights-based perspective. However, to many conservationists it will seem like an obviously good thing. Conservationists seek to preserve species or populations rather than individuals. For some, this is because species are regarded as valuable for their contribution to human happiness. But it is also a key area of disagreement between rights theorists and environmental philosophers, some of whom locate value in systems or collectives rather than individuals.

Other common justifications for zoos are that they are educational and provide opportunities for research. Zoos offer a way to learn about the natural world and the animals in it and may encourage people to show them more concern. This justification makes us consider whether it is right to sacrifice animal interests for the sake of knowledge, especially when that knowledge is not new and can be gained in other ways. This, like the previous justification, illustrates the difference between rights-based and consequentialist approaches to ethics. The rights view says that benefits are not sufficient to justify violating rights.

Despite the arguments against zoos, even within an animal rights framework, it might be possible for zoos to continue. Often, zoos take animals rescued from poachers, animal traffickers, circuses or irresponsible pet owners. These animals may have been subjected to treatment, or grown up in conditions, that make it difficult to release them without harm. In such cases, a zoo might be able to provide a safe and therapeutic environment. Other animals can enjoy high welfare in zoo conditions without their rights being violated. In a world where animal rights are respected, we would rarely be able to see elephants or primates in a zoo, and the conditions for animals within zoos would be even more stringently regulated, but zoos need not disappear altogether. An animal-rights respecting zoo would much more closely resemble an animal sanctuary than the zoos we are familiar with today.

## Animal experimentation

Cruelty Free International estimates that every year almost two hundred million animals are used for scientific purposes. This includes nearly eighty million experiments on animals, as well as millions of other animals who are killed for their tissue or used to breed genetically modified animal strains, and those who are bred but not used. Figures are difficult to estimate precisely, however, and the true total is likely to be significantly higher. This is because countries such as the US, which reports close to eight hundred thousand animals used in research per year, do not include birds, rats, mice or fish in their figures. Although rats, mice and fish are the most common animals experimented upon, America's Animal Welfare Act (AWA) does not class these species as animals and so does not require reporting of tests done on them. Acts like the AWA are designed to conceal the nature and extent of animal experimentation and are part of a culture of secrecy in this field.

Animal experimentation refers to procedures performed on living animals for research and teaching purposes, such as to learn about diseases and biology. It also includes the testing of medical and commercial products such as cosmetics, cleaning products and food. Not all tests are physical; many are psychological. For example, one of the reasons we know so much about the harmful effects of loneliness, maternal deprivation and isolation in humans is because of experiments carried out on social nonhuman animals.

Some of the most infamous of these were carried out in the 1950s and 1960s by the behavioural scientists Harry and Margaret Harlow. In one experiment, the Harlows separated infant monkeys from their mothers and provided cloth-and-wire surrogates in their place. The purpose of this research was to make breeding monkeys for experimentation easier: 'By separating them from their mothers a few hours after birth and placing them in a more fully controlled regimen of nurture and physical care we were able both to achieve a higher rate of survival and to remove the animals for testing without maternal protest.'[11] Instead, they discovered that the infants they'd separated from their mothers grew up with serious psychological problems:

> The laboratory-born monkeys sit in their cages and stare fixedly into space, circle their cages in a repetitive stereotyped manner and clasp their heads in their hands or arms and rock for long periods of time. They often develop compulsive habits, such as pinching precisely the same patch of skin on the chest between the same fingers hundreds of times a day; occasionally such behavior may become punitive and the animal may chew and tear at its body until it bleeds.

Having observed this phenomenon, the Harlows devised a series of even crueller experiments to measure the effects of psychological trauma. One of these, which Harry Harlow nicknamed 'The Pit of Despair', involved isolating young monkeys for three months at a time until they broke down. Its intent was to cause depression. Another contained a forced mating device that he called 'The Rape Rack'. The Harlows' aim was to 'point the way to reducing the toll of psychosocial trauma in human society'. They sought to benefit humanity, but they did so without any regard for the monkeys in their care.

The Harlows received numerous accolades for their research, with Harry awarded a national medal of science and made president of the American Psychological Association (APA), although the APA eventually shut down his research in the 1980s on

**Figure 4.3: Harry Harlow with infant monkey on wire surrogate**

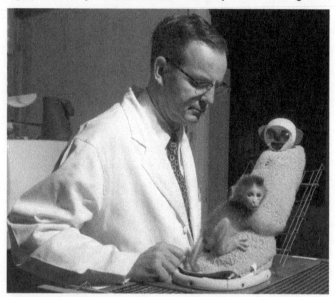

Infamous research by the psychologist Harry Harlow revealed that monkeys suffer severe psychological problems when separated from their mothers as infants or when kept in long-term isolation. By causing depression in monkeys, and through deliberate maternal deprivation, Harlow hoped to learn about human psychology.

ethical grounds. Ethical regimes around animal experimentation are much stricter today, but there are still countries that provide little or no protection to animals used in scientific research.

Many tests are carried out on nonhuman animals because the law requires it, particularly in the case of medicines. Products are tested for toxicity by injection, ingestion or exposure; animals are subjected to unnecessary surgery; have wounds inflicted to

## Box 4.2: Rules on the use of animals in research

There is no internationally agreed standard or law governing
the use of nonhuman animals in scientific research. The only
international standard and system of accreditation is run by
a private, nonprofit organization. Nevertheless, much of the
legislation that exists is informed by what are known as the
3Rs: replacement, reduction and refinement. These principles
were developed and then outlined in the late 1950s by
the biologists William Russell and Rex Burch in their book
*The Principle of Humane Experimentation Technique*.[12] The
3Rs stress the importance of avoiding or reducing the use
of animals (replacement); minimizing the numbers used
consistent with the aims of the research (reduction); and
minimizing the pain, suffering, distress or lasting harm caused
to the animals used (refinement).

The most developed legal system is that of the European
Union, which has recognition of animal sentience built into
Article 13 of the Treaty of Lisbon and the intrinsic value of
sentient beings in the Directive on the Protection of Animals
Used for Scientific Purposes (2010/63/EU). EU law requires
member states to have consistent standards of housing,
training, care and regulation, which embody the 3Rs. In
other legal jurisdictions, standards and laws vary wildly. As
in the US, often the most commonly experimented on animals
are excluded from legal protections. Many countries differ
on the degree to which practices are regulated centrally,
with countries like Australia and Japan devolving matters to

federal levels or self-governance by individual organizations respectively. Elsewhere, in much of Africa, Latin America and the Middle East, there are few laws on animal experimentation and little or no governance or oversight.

study healing; are caused pain to study pain relief and physiology; are given conditions such as strokes or cancer; are inflicted with disabilities to study their ability to cope; are subjected to restraint and deprivation in psychological tests; and are genetically manipulated to add or remove genes. Increasingly, nonhuman animals are also being genetically manipulated and cloned to provide body parts for human use. For example, pigs have been engineered to produce skin for burn victims, bio-compatible hearts for humans, corneas, and insulin.

Often, procedures are ranked by degree of harmfulness to the animal, and the law requires that suffering be minimized where possible. Before beginning experiments, researchers must obtain permission from a regulatory body, and many procedures are now outlawed. For example, testing cosmetics on nonhuman animals is no longer permitted in the European Union. However, many of the experiments that continue to be carried out cause a great deal of harm and distress. Although most animals are killed at the end of an experiment, some are first subjected to multiple procedures. Most animals experimented on have been bred for the purpose and so experience nothing beyond the laboratory in their lives.

From an animal rights perspective, what should we think about scientific procedures? The first thing to say is that the enforcement of animal rights would probably not completely rule out experimentation. The examples of experiments I have given are the sort that cause serious harm and represent the use of nonhuman animals merely to serve human interest. These experiments violate important animal interests against suffering, and in life, bodily integrity and health. As a result, they cannot easily be justified. Nevertheless, it's possible to imagine some uses of animals in research that do not cause them harm and may be carried out for the benefit of the animals themselves. Under a rights view, these experiments are permissible.

The usual response to the animal rights view is to point to the benefits that come from scientific research. These kinds of arguments often take two forms. One is to argue that nonhuman animals, although worthy of consideration, are lesser beings and therefore can be used to promote human interests. Another is to take a consequentialist approach. Consequentialist ethical theories, of which utilitarianism is one, say that acts are justified in terms of their consequences. This is different from theories that say acts are justified based on, for example, the intentions behind them or their conformity to a moral rule, such as promise-keeping. Consequentialists argue that the harms done to nonhuman animals are justified by the benefits to humans. To help justify animal experimentation, people contend that although harming animals might be bad, it is necessary to obtain the benefits scientists seek.

There are several replies that can be made to these arguments. Recall that, in Chapter 2, I introduced you to the letter from Porphyry to his friend Firmus Cystericus, in which he pointed out that just because humans possess certain capacities to a higher degree than other animals doesn't mean that other animals lack those capacities. The conclusion we can take from Porphyry is that even if it is true that nonhumans are worthy of less moral concern than humans, it wouldn't follow that we can do what we wish to them. Given a forced choice between saving a human and saving a cat, I would save the human, but this doesn't mean that I am therefore permitted to torture the cat, or to kill it and eat it if I like the taste of cats.

People often think of experimentation as like a forced choice situation, where we must choose between saving the human or the cat. This is because animal experimentation is presented as necessary to prevent serious harms to humans. But the analogy doesn't quite hold. Forced choices in ethics refer to cases where we must choose between two or more ethically unpalatable options. In these cases, agents must choose the lesser evil. But, in many cases, it isn't clear that the harms done to nonhuman animals are indeed the lesser of the evils, particularly if it is true that they possess rights. This is especially clear if the benefit to humans is limited and the cost to nonhumans high.

Second, the idea of necessity in this sort of argument serves to cloud the matter. In this case, saying that experiments are necessary doesn't mean that there is no choice. Rather, it means that the results being sought cannot be as easily or affordably obtained in other ways. Sometimes that means the economic costs of alternatives are too high or the technology required to carry out the science without animals isn't yet available. For this line of argument to succeed, it first must be shown that it is permissible to seriously harm nonhuman animals for the sake of benefiting humans which, as we know, the animal rights view rejects. The rights view is that any benefits obtained in this way are impermissible. In other words, it is morally impermissible to violate rights to gain benefits.

Rather than being a choice of which being to save, the case of experimentation is, at least for some medical research, more analogous to one where we must choose whether to kill one human to save another. Some people would be prepared to kill a stranger to save a loved one if their loved one required an organ they cannot otherwise obtain. However, just because individuals may think this justified does not make it right. While our loved ones are more important to us than strangers, the law ought to regard everyone as equally worthy of protection.

Similarly, it is not morally permissible to clone humans to harvest their organs, even if doing so would benefit more humans than are cloned. Nor would it become permissible to do this to cloned humans if scientists somehow, through genetic manipulation, made those cloned humans barely rational. Even if we were pure utilitarians, we would both need to include the suffering of nonhuman animals in our utility calculus, and to show that whatever experiment we wished to pursue was the best way to maximize utility. Given how much more efficient it would be to direct money at preventing suffering by distributing food and existing medicines and improving sanitation, it's hard to see how it could be.

5

# EMERGING ISSUES: FROM MOLLUSC RIGHTS TO ANIMAL CITIZENS

The case studies above each address longstanding issues in animal rights. More recent topics of research can help identify both the limits of rights as a mechanism for protecting interests and their potential to offer a radically different vision of the future. The first of these emerging issues concerns the significance of invertebrate suffering.

## Insects, molluscs, crustaceans and the precautionary principle

Earlier, we looked at the possibility of animal agriculture continuing in some form by using creatures that lack sentience. Some practices that would seem abhorrent if done to creatures that can feel might not be at all troubling if done to non-sentient beings. For example, one ubiquitous practice in aquaculture is known as eye ablation. Farmers have discovered that female shrimp spawn more quickly if they are blinded. As a result, farmers usually pinch or cut off one or both eyestalks. Meanwhile, crustaceans are routinely boiled alive in many parts of the world, and intensive octopus farming is seen a profitable new industry. If invertebrates cannot feel, then they will not have rights and it is hard to see how death and injury directly wrong them. However, just as we now know that fish are sentient, studies have shown that many invertebrates are too.

## Box 5.1: Fish and invertebrate sentience

For a long time, it was believed that fish, insects, most molluscs and crustaceans lacked sentience. Scientists maintained that these creatures only possessed nociception, a physiological response to a noxious stimulus. (As an example of nociception, if you accidentally touch something very hot, you will find that your body shrinks away from the source of heat in the brief moment before you begin to feel pain. The shrinking away is an instinctive, subconscious reaction that occurs before any conscious awareness of pain.) Studies have now shown that not only are fish sentient, but many invertebrates are too.

In the case of fish, there is both physiological and behavioural evidence for sentience.[1] Fish have areas of the brain that appear to govern emotions, and that show electrical activity during exposure to noxious stimuli. Experiments have been devised to test whether animals learn to avoid noxious stimuli or make sacrifices to do so, and if they have bodily responses consistent with awareness of pain. For example, introducing acetic acid to their environment results in zebrafish decreasing their activity, behaviour that is reversed when pain relief medicine is introduced. Similarly, goldfish learn to avoid areas of their environment where they have received an electric shock, even when those places are known to also contain food. Some fish even seem able to pass the mirror test.[2] The evidence points to something beyond nociception: it points to awareness, to pain.

The same experiments have been carried out on octopi with similar results. When injected with acetic acid, octopi perform grooming behaviours on the affected site, and respond positively to the subsequent application of anaesthetic.[3] There is also a growing body of evidence pointing to sentience in different species of decapod crustaceans (lobsters, crabs, shrimp and so on),[4] and perhaps in insects too.[5] Bees, for example, have been shown to make motivational trade-offs between sources of food and the presence of noxious stimuli (such as high heat) in ways that suggest a capacity to feel pain.[6]

If science demonstrates the existence of negative emotions in these creatures, they too ought to be granted rights, and practices such as those described previously should be outlawed. In the case of insects, the science on sentience is more limited and less conclusive. As a result, some argue that it is permissible to continue treating them as though they are not sentient.

**Figure 5.1:** *Octopus vulgaris,* **the common octopus**

Octopi are not only sentient, but curious, imaginative and remarkably intelligent. Plans by a Spanish seafood company, uncovered in 2023, to build the first intensive octopus farm would cause serious suffering. Scientific research has shown that sentience exists in a far wider range of creatures than we used to believe.

Others say that we should adopt a precautionary principle.[7] In the case of sentience, this states that where there is the possibility of sentience in a creature, we ought to act as if that creature were sentient until science settles the matter. The reason for this is that if we act as if the creature is not sentient, and it later turns out that we were wrong, then we will have caused enormous pain. If we act as if the creature is sentient and it turns out that they are not, then we will merely have temporarily deprived ourselves of a benefit but done no lasting harm. Better to mistakenly do no harm than to mistakenly do harm. Given the numbers of insects, crustaceans and molluscs farmed, the harm we risk doing by mistakenly assuming non-sentience is substantial.

## Animals in the wild

Another important question concerns what we owe to wild animals. Humans have a huge impact on the habitats of wild animals. We have disrupted and devastated ecosystems, radically altered the environment and greatly reduced the amount of space available for nonhuman animals to live and roam within. Often, conservation policies and public concern focus on the importance of ecosystems and biodiversity for human health and happiness. In other words, policies are directed at saving species and habitats for anthropocentric reasons rather than protecting the rights of individual animals. But, if nonhuman animals have rights protecting their vital interests, then destroying habitats count as an injustice towards them. Many nonhuman animals cannot satisfy their preferences and live good lives outside their natural habitats. Some species require unique and vulnerable habitats simply to survive. Under an interest theory of rights, those animals deserve to have the interests they have in living in particular habitats protected. This means that issues like deforestation, pollution and anthropogenic climate change aren't only wrong because they harm humans. Environmental destruction of habitats also costs the lives of countless wild animals. As a result, acting in ways that knowingly, deliberately and avoidably damage the environment can be wrong because such acts violate the habitat rights of wild animals.

It might be possible to respect the rights of wild animals by simply leaving them and their habitats alone. But might we also have duties to assist them when they are in need? Suppose a habitat is threatened by a natural disaster such as a drought. It isn't all that implausible to think that a commitment to animal rights would require us to offer some aid to suffering animals. A duty to aid others in dire need corresponds to their having what I referred to at the end of Chapter 3 as a positive right. However, following this intuition through to its logical conclusion leads to what is known as 'the predation problem'.

Imagine you are walking home one day and you see someone kicking a dog. What should you do? Many people's first instinct would be to intervene to halt the attack. We might explain this by saying that the dog's right is being violated and that bystanders have duties to intervene in such cases. Now imagine instead you encounter a fox about to pounce on a rabbit. Are you obliged to intervene in this case? To think that humans ought to intervene to prevent predation seems very counterintuitive. So much so that examples like that of the fox and rabbit are used to try to show that the animal rights position leads to ridiculous conclusions (what is known as a *reductio ad absurdum* argument, or *reductio* for short).

At first glance, it seems like the poor rabbit is having their right against being harmed violated by the fox. However, this is not the case. Rights can only be violated by the acts of moral agents. Even though the fox harms the rabbit, it isn't the case that the fox violates the rabbit's rights because the fox is unable to act differently. The fox no more violates the rabbit's right than a falling tree or an extremely cold winter might.

Unfortunately, the predation problem is not so easy to solve as that. This is because many rights theorists think that rights-holders hold both negative and positive rights. Not only must we avoid violating rights, we must also assist others in dire need, because rights-holders possess a right to assistance. If that is so, then although the fox does not violate the rabbit's negative right, humans may violate the rabbit's positive right by failing to rescue them. Since the fox cannot live without killing rabbits, we would be harming the fox if we did so. Things look difficult, not just for the rabbit but also for rights theorists.

One solution to the predation problem is to claim that we may owe humans positive rights, but not nonhuman animals. In other words, nonhuman animals only have negative rights: rights against interference. But why think that humans and nonhuman animals are different enough to merit this? Such differential treatment seems arbitrary and thus speciesist. Two obvious routes to avoid this charge are open to the defender of animal rights. One is to argue that nobody has positive rights, neither humans nor nonhumans. In such a world, we would have to leave one another alone, but nobody would be required to provide assistance to others.

If we take that route, it's hard to see how any rights could be enforced, and so rights would lose all power. A more plausible version of the argument is to claim that we only have positive rights to assistance when our negative rights are being violated. A world where we adopt this view is even more alien and radical than one where animals are granted rights: it comes without a right to education, healthcare or welfare of any sort.

A second way to avoid the predation problem is to argue that what we owe to wild animals is different from what we owe to domesticated animals. We might think that our long history of making domesticated animals vulnerable and dependent upon us generates special duties towards them that are absent in the case of wild animals. Unlike domesticated animals, wild animals should be let be.[8] This approach is the one most animal rights theorists have leaned towards. One issue with it is that if we are to be consistent in our principles, it also appears to require adopting a similar stance towards human strangers in dire need.

The predation problem can be overcome using the strategies outlined here, but only with difficulty. Utilitarians tend to have an easier time thinking ethically about wild animals than rights-theorists. For them, the question of how to deal with issues like predation concerns how much suffering living wild produces. If there are actions available to us that would limit that suffering, then we may be required to take them. Utilitarians look for ways to respond to wild animal suffering that maximize the amount of happiness in the world. Unfortunately, the simplicity of utilitarian principles can lead to its own counter-intuitive conclusions. For example, given that vast numbers of wild animals die young and in pain, one way to minimize wild animal suffering might be to do away with the wilderness altogether. Thus, some utilitarians argue for much more interventionist management of ecosystems, including taking steps to eliminate predation, disease, parasitism, hunger and so forth. Not only does this seem absurd to many people, it would be likely to have profound and unpredictable consequences.

## Animal citizens

Rights issues around wild animals are tricky, but (thanks to humans) wild animals only make up a tiny proportion of land animals. For example, of all the mammals on earth, only 4 per cent are wild mammals. Sixty per cent of land mammals are livestock, and around 36 per cent are humans. Meanwhile, only around 30 per cent of birds live wild; the majority are farmed poultry.[9] Most of the world's land animals live within human communities. So, in the final section of this chapter, I want to briefly look at what animal rights might mean for the composition of political communities such as states.

Members of a political community possess certain rights and entitlements against other members of the community and against its political authority. These are known as citizenship rights. Citizens of a state ought to have a say in how the state is governed, be protected by the state, have a right to live in the state and have freedom to obtain all the other benefits that come from being part of a collective. Non-citizens may have rights within states above the minimum standard of universal human rights, but they are restricted. Non-citizens, such as tourists and migrant workers, lack a right to participate in the governance of the state and to access a full range of benefits. Recently, animal rights theorists have begun to propose that some nonhuman animals ought to be considered as citizens, particularly those forcibly brought into our communities via domestication and made dependent on us. Those animals, it is argued, can live in harmony with humans, engage in mutually beneficial activities and cooperate, and so should be entitled to the special rights associated with membership.[10]

For example, we've seen how companion animals are often regarded as members of the family, so they already inhabit the same mental space as citizens in the minds of many people. Similarly, many people believe that service animals, such as police dogs, ought to receive special rights in recognition for the dangers they face and the contribution they make towards keeping citizens safe. In 2016, UK police dog Finn was stabbed when his handler confronted a suspected criminal. Finn required emergency surgery and was later given several awards for his service. Finn's attacker could not be prosecuted for assaulting Finn. Instead, he faced a charge of criminal damage to police property – the dog. The incident prompted a campaign for changes to the law, and harming a service animal was made a specific offence as a result. Although service animals in the UK still lack legal standing in their own rights, the debates around Finn's law demonstrated that many people regarded service animals as worthy of special protection for their sakes and as legal persons.

In practice, citizenship rights for nonhumans might mean that working animals receive entitlements to worker benefits and protections. These might include retirement rights, rights to healthcare, time off, limits to working hours, health and safety protections, and perhaps even wages (paid into a trust tasked with acting on their behalf). Of course, it would also need to be true that nonhuman animals were not harmed by their professions, that they demonstrated some willingness to work and were able to enjoy a good standard of welfare. With citizenship rights, life for service animals, guide dogs, guard dogs, therapy animals, and horses used for riding or pulling carriages would be very different. More widely, animal citizens would be entitled to have their interests represented in political institutions. This might mean, for example, animal advocates with constitutional roles and democratic structures, like citizen juries, set up to discern and advance animal interests. Institutional arrangements of these sorts present problems, such as that of balancing the interests of different animals and of discerning those interests in the first place. However, they are not insurmountable.

In the next chapter, I explore how rights function in moral deliberation and campaigns such as that for Finn's Law.

6

# ENGAGING THE IMAGINATION: TURNING PREJUDICE INTO COMPASSION

Philosophical thinking has been a crucial part of the quest for animal rights. Some have even argued that philosophers acted as midwives to a social movement for animal rights.[1] Social movements are collectives working together in pursuit of a common goal and with a shared sense of identity. To build social movements, it is necessary to develop that shared identity and goal, and in this respect the concept of rights is a powerful tool. In this chapter, I explain how philosophical thinking about moral concepts, values and principles is helpful for the animal rights cause, and how it also highlights some limitations. To do this, I explore aspects of moral psychology – how we reason about morality – and its connection both with individual decision-making and the building of political movements. The most important theme of the chapter is the link between animal rights and the role played by the imagination in ethics.

One of the driving forces behind the animal rights movement is emotion. Activists are motivated to become vegan and to campaign for animal rights out of a sense of compassion for suffering animals. Compassion is the emotion of fellow feeling. When we feel compassion for another, we begin by imagining ourselves in their situation and take their perspective. If we judge that whatever is afflicting them is bad, we are moved to feel compassion. Conversely, if we judge that they deserve whatever pain they feel, then the force of our compassion will be blunted. In other words, compassion includes taking the perspective of another and making a moral judgement about their suffering. Compassion is an emotion with an evaluative component that depends on use of the imagination.

Compassion is powerfully motivating because it accompanies moral judgement with an awareness that pain is profoundly negative for whoever is experiencing it. So, animal rights campaigns try to engage the imagination by drawing attention to suffering. Often, people turn to veganism and the acceptance of animal rights after a formative experience; a sudden realization causes them to shift their world view. Frequently, this moment comes from exposure to a shocking image, account or video about the treatment of nonhuman animals. Campaigning approaches that provoke shock, disgust or horror are successful because humans are psychologically disposed to respond more forcefully to negative events or feelings.[2] However, those negative emotions also need to be accompanied by a moral judgement, otherwise the emotions merely serve to drive people away from their source.

One way that the concept of rights can function is to help us make the evaluations necessary for compassion. This is because rights are a familiar way of thinking about our moral and political relationships. The concept of rights is embedded in our legal, social and political culture, and forms a central element of our moral vocabulary. If someone claims that animals deserve rights, we know straight away that this means we should treat them in particular ways. If we say that a right is being violated, we instinctively know that the matter is important and that an injustice is at stake.

The use of familiar concepts helps us to reason in unfamiliar contexts: they function as heuristics – mental shortcuts that help us to avoid being overcome by the cognitive load needed to make decisions. When we reason about what we ought to do, we face a great many barriers to good decision-making. For example, limited information, cognitive biases, situational complexity, tiredness and time constraints all hinder our reasoning ability. With so many obstacles, if we were to carefully consider the moral status of all our options all the time, we would be overwhelmed. One example of a heuristic used to overcome these constraints is trust. When deciding how to act, rather than performing a complex evaluation, people will often act in the same way as someone they trust. For example, when making judgements about how to respond to pandemics, most people lack the scientific skills to evaluate the evidence for themselves. Instead, they trust the judgement of experts, particularly those they are familiar with, such as famous doctors or scientists. Heuristics help us to make sense of the world and make rapid judgements.

The goal of animal rights campaigns is to convince us that the suffering of animals is morally wrong, and that helps to explain why centring campaigns on rights can be a useful strategy. As we saw in Chapter 2, animal rights are a moral concept. When we say that a nonhuman animal has rights, we are making a claim that there are strong moral reasons to protect their interests and that these generate duties. Talking about moral entitlements in terms of rights is familiar and part of many cultures. So, when campaigners assert that animal have rights and accompany this claim with examples of suffering, people will have been primed to consider that suffering in moral terms. Making animal suffering a rights issue can act as a heuristic, laying the groundwork for a compassionate response.

## Building a movement: animal rights as a political ideology

Heuristics aren't just useful for making rapid moral judgements about how to act. In addition to this function, they play a role in understanding and categorizing the world, and in orienting us in relation to it. In social and political contexts, ideologies act as one such heuristic. Ideologies are structured sets of beliefs and values about how society ought to be ordered. Being able to connect beliefs or values with an ideology enables us to quickly categorize them and to understand where they sit in relation to other beliefs. Having an identifiable ideology makes it easier for people to coalesce, campaign and coordinate around value issues. Over time, the animal rights movement has begun to turn into an ideology,[3] with the idea that nonhuman animals are rights-holders, protected by principles of justice, at its core. Today, there are even political parties, such as the Dutch Party for the Animals, German Animal Protection Party and the Animal Justice Party of Finland, which stand primarily on an animal rights platform. In countries with proportional representation, these parties have won seats in local, regional, national and European Union elections. In 2021 the Dutch Party for the Animals won close to 4 per cent of the national vote.

One way the animal rights ideology is often characterized is by distinguishing it from an animal welfare approach. Although the boundaries between them are fuzzy, the animal welfare approach focuses on improving conditions for nonhuman animals without challenging the basic structures and practices that enable their use. For example, a welfarist response to animal agriculture is to seek to reduce the cruelty of factory farming without doing away with the killing and consumption of animals. Similarly, an example of welfarism in animal research is the 3Rs framework, which calls for the gradual reduction, refinement and

**Figure 6.1: Animal rights as ideology**

The idea that nonhuman animals are owed rights can be thought of as an ideology. Ideologies serve as ways of mentally grouping concepts and values, enabling us to quickly make decisions about how to act and to evaluate situations and claims. An animal rights ideology says that nonhuman animals are valuable for their own sakes and owed legal protections in their own rights. Political parties for animal rights have tended to reject animal ownership and have broader commitments to a philosophy of equality, compassion and environmental protection.

replacement of nonhuman animals rather for a ban on their use. Welfarism aims to reduced harm, the rights approach aims to eliminate it.

Throughout the history of animal welfare and rights, strands of the movement have been bound up with other causes such as working-class, feminist and environmental issues. More recently, the animal rights movement has taken on a more distinct identity and purpose, though many campaigners continue to connect the oppression of nonhuman animals with other forms of oppression. The distinction between welfare approaches and rights approaches is an important means of understanding and identifying the modern movement, and it is frequently asserted that it is what distinguishes the post-1970s movement from earlier ones. This distinction is also sometimes described in terms of welfarist vs liberationist, or welfarist vs abolitionist. However it is described, the distinction serves to highlight that calls for animal rights are far more radical than welfarist concerns and that they represent an ideological platform rather than a single issue campaign.

As mentioned earlier, one of the aims of the animal rights movement, and the centrepiece of its ideology, has been to show that our treatment of nonhuman animals is a matter of justice. One of the roles played by the idea of animal rights is to highlight that the treatment of other animals is both important and a matter of political morality. To do this, campaigners have drawn analogies with the struggles of oppressed groups of humans. Arguments from analogy attempt to show that two cases are morally alike in some relevant respect. Usually, this is done by showing that the principles governing moral judgements in a familiar case apply in the same way to an unfamiliar one. Through comparison, analogies can act as a form of heuristic. Use of the term 'speciesism', along with the argument from awkward cases, aims to show that the treatment of nonhuman animals is both arbitrary and unjust in similar ways to other familiar forms of discrimination. Such arguments are intended to show that we ought to extend rights to other species because the grounds of rights are the same for humans as for other animals.

In addition to highlighting inconsistencies in our moral principles, campaigners have made use of the language of justice and injustice. Besides rights talk, terms like 'liberation', '(in)justice', 'oppression' and 'exploitation' mark out the movement as political in nature and help us to mentally categorize it as a particular kind of struggle. Singer's *Animal Liberation* has been successful not just because the arguments within it are compelling, but also because it provides readers with a clear picture of the harms done to nonhuman animals, employing the language of political liberation. It begins: 'This book is about the tyranny of human over non-human animals', and immediately follows this by making a comparison with racial oppression.[4] Similarly, the influence of Bentham's famous passage (set out in Chapter 2) can partly be explained by the powerful prose and the analogies he draws: 'The day may come, when the rest of the animal creation may acquire those rights which never could have been withholden from them but by the hand of tyranny.' In each case, the term 'tyranny' shows that the authors regard this as a matter of political morality requiring a collective response.

The quote from Bentham is helpful because it is directed towards a vision of a better future: 'The day may come ...'. Here, we can draw on the idea of moral progress to help explain the role played by animal rights. Moral progress describes the idea that it is possible to make moral improvements to our world in a gradual and sustained way. If we can make moral progress then, over time, we will move closer and closer to an ideal society, one where laws much more closely match the requirements of justice. Recall that in Chapter 2 I described how moral rights function as a means of thinking about the future, and about how laws ought to govern our societies. For animal rights theorists, the ideal society might look like the one I described in the introduction to this book, one where animals have their vital interests protected by rights and are able to live good, flourishing lives alongside humans.

A key question for political philosophers is how moral progress can be achieved. One important theory is that progress is made by learning to appreciate the world in new ways. This approach to progress takes the view that information about how we ought to act is already available to us and can be described using familiar moral concepts. Rather than needing to uncover new truths and invent new concepts, we must learn to appreciate what is already before us and to apply our existing concepts in new ways.[5] This approach to moral progress accords well with the one taken by animal rights theorists, who attempt to apply political concepts such as rights, equality, freedom, citizenship, justice and democracy to nonhuman animals.

## Thinking ethically

In the previous discussion of compassion, we saw that the imagination plays a role in deciding how to respond to another's pain. We also explored how the use of heuristics to aid decision-making is often necessary because of limits on our powers of reason. In fact, the imagination plays an even wider role than I've so far described, because moral decision-making, by its nature, involves evaluating options and making choices. When faced with an ethical decision, we use our imaginations to play out possible courses of action, identify ethically salient facts and compare the merits of the options open to us. Similarly, when making moral judgements about what others have done, we imagine what else they might have done instead. If we can imagine a better course of action than the one they took, we might think their action blameworthy, and if we think they could not have acted better, then we praise them.

Humans, however, cannot contemplate every possible option. There are psychological limits on how many choices we can consider. Instead, we first identify the most plausible options and then compare a narrow range of them.[6] These features of our ethical decision-making process can make it difficult to accept animal rights. One reason that I used examples in Chapter 4 of what animal rights mean in practice is that it can be difficult to imagine societies very different from our own. When we imagine how things might be, we do so by resorting to familiar concepts, structures and associations. To imagine a fantastical creature, it is easier to picture a hybrid of an eagle and a horse, such as a griffin or Pegasus, than it is to conjure up an entirely original being.

Similar difficulties occur when trying to describe new political communities. If a possible political community has very different political structures and social relationships, it is difficult to picture. A society where ownership of nonhuman animals is not permitted; where nonhuman animals are citizens, with similar labour, political and welfare rights to humans; and where animal representatives are included in constitutional and democratic processes can be hard to imagine. As a result, animal rights are likely to be excluded from the range of possible options we deliberate over when contemplating the society we ought build. Such a society seems too far-fetched or fantastical.[7]

When we reason about justice in ideal societies, we do so by drawing on familiar moral and political concepts. The bigger the difference of a utopian vision from our own society, the harder it is to imagine and the less likely it is to be accepted as a believable alternative. This means that if familiar concepts and moral principles are not present in an imagined utopia, it will be harder to motivate people to strive to achieve it. Part of the role of philosophers and campaigners for animal rights is therefore to show that familiar concepts and principles *can* be applied across species to make justice for nonhuman animals believable. However, there are limits to how successful this can be.

Concepts are ways of mentally representing entities and the world. A good concept identifies the key features of the thing it describes in a coherent way and can be applied across a range of cases. Concepts allow us to distinguish between things in useful ways. However, some of the concepts that are core to our systems of moral thought are quite difficult to apply in nonhuman cases. Some, like dignity, are usually theorized in terms of the capacity for reason, or feelings of shame, self-esteem and pride, which means that they need extensive work to be applied to nonhuman animals. Similarly, many rights depend for their moral force on the capacity for autonomy. 'Autonomy' is a word with two meanings. In one sense, autonomy describes the capacity to act without external guidance. Thus, we can talk meaningfully of autonomous robots or weapons systems. In another, morally relevant, sense, autonomy is about the capacity to make choices that are contrary to one's desires. The second sense of autonomy originates in the work of Kant (see Chapter 2) and is used by philosophers to describe what makes moral agency possible. It is this that rights such as freedom of choice, political self-determination and freedom of conscience seek to protect. Because nonhuman animals lack a developed capacity for autonomy in the second sense, associated rights and moral concepts, such as personhood, cannot easily be deployed in moral discourse about them. Other rights, like equality, run up against a deeply engrained preference for our own species that is both psychological and cultural. Additionally, feeling compassion for some animals may be a struggle because it is difficult to imagine what it is like to be them. The fewer similarities we can identify between ourselves and another species, the harder it is to imagine how they feel. Feeling compassion for weird, ugly and alien creatures is much harder than feeling it for another ape.[8]

It may be that there is a biological explanation for these difficulties sympathizing with other species. Evolutionary psychologists have argued that humans have evolved to show preference for kin as a way of increasing the chance of our survival and genetic propagation. This kin preference manifests in what have been described as concentric circles or spheres of concern. Our loved ones exist in the circle of concern closest to us, and others in circles spaced gradually further apart. The further away from the centre point, either in imaginative or geographical terms, the less our concern. Hence, it is often harder to sympathize with distant strangers (or alien-seeming nonhuman animals) than neighbours.

Evolutionary biology might provide a good explanation for why people often behave the way they do, but it only helps a little when thinking about how they *should* act. Partiality may be natural but, from a moral point of view, my loved ones are no more important than anyone else's. All humans possess an equal basic value regardless of how much you or I personally care about them. Although it may often be the right thing to do to treat one's loved ones preferentially, that doesn't mean we should always do so, or that we should disregard the interests of strangers. Part of the project of ethics is to overcome our natural tendencies and biases, including those towards our own species. Ethicists sometimes describe this as expanding the circle of concern, which we can think of as coming to care more about the wellbeing of those distant or different from us.[9] One advantage of thinking in terms of rights is that rights signify that our preferences aren't relevant to another being's entitlements. Just because we don't like someone or are indifferent to their wellbeing does not mean that we ought to be free to treat them however we wish. If they have a right, we must treat them a certain way regardless of what we desire. So, although it may be difficult to feel motivated to protect the welfare of unlikeable animals, a claim that they have rights tells us that our personal attitude is irrelevant to their status from a moral point of view.

## Problems with rights-talk

Because contemporary campaigns for the better treatment of nonhuman animals often make use of rights-talk, they are also vulnerable to wider problems associated with rights. These include ethical and theoretical concerns about the concept of rights in general. One additional practical problem is that animal rights have negative associations and provoke hostility in some people. Let us begin with the practical problem – animal rights are an unpopular idea – before moving on to wider issues with rights.

Many studies have shown that veganism attracts prejudice and hostility. That hostility varies depending on the reasons given for veganism. Least hostility is felt towards those who profess health or environmental reasons for veganism, while the greatest hostility is reserved for those who are vegan on animal rights grounds.[10] Why is that, and what does it mean for animal rights campaigners? A big part of the answer concerns the connection between values and identity.

When we think about who we are, and how others regard us, the values that we hold form a big part of our identity. Imagine that someone known for being peaceful, honest and generous suffers a brain injury that causes them to become aggressive, deceitful and selfish. Even if they retained all their memories, we might regard them as almost being a different person.[11] The values we hold are core to our sense of self, and that's why being asked to change them can feel frightening. Animal rights represent a challenge to the value system of most people. Being told to accept that animals have rights is the same as being told to change one's values, and thus to change an aspect of one's identity. For some groups, the identities they hold are particularly hostile to animal rights views. Conservatives and communitarians, for example, place high value on conformity and community. As a result, minority groups with different values and customs are perceived as an existential threat, and this helps to explain why right-wing views are often hostile to animal rights.[12]

Similarly, as mentioned in Chapter 1, the use and consumption of nonhuman animals is associated with luxury, health and strength, and particularly masculinity. Because of these associations, vegans are frequently and unfairly stereotyped as joyless[13] and unhealthy. At the same time, the association of meat-eating, particularly red meat, with strength and masculinity feeds into patriarchal worldviews. Meat-eating is thought of as manly and veganism effeminate. Because behaviours, attributes and values associated with femininity are valued less highly than those linked with masculinity, animal rights views suffer a sort of sexism-by-proxy. This prejudice has been exacerbated by the fact that animal protection movements have historically had a higher proportion of women than men in them, and because these have also been tied up with other social and political campaigns, such as women's rights. These associations have been present throughout the modern history of animal rights and animal welfare, with campaigners often accused of being overly emotional and irrational – traits negatively associated with women. As a result of these negative associations, the concept of animal rights may struggle to gain purchase, and its use will cause some groups to reject greater protections for nonhuman animals. To overcome this, activists could approach hostile groups with a different strategy, such as for more gradual change couched in terms of benefits to humans. While pushing for more gradual change seems at odds with the rights-based approach of this book, pragmatically it may be the only way to gain enough political momentum to make genuinely radical changes. Alternatively (or at the same time), activists need to find ways to challenge the broader prejudices before they can make progress on animal rights.

Another important and more radical criticism came from the twentieth-century British philosopher Mary Midgley. Midgley asserted that rights might be the wrong way of talking about our moral relations altogether. She claimed that concepts like obligations, duties, rights and justice have narrowed so much in meaning that they are imagined as only applying in the context of contracts between free and rational agents.[14] Furthermore, she argued that the model of rationality at work in social contract theory is based on a false binary: rationality is regarded as being either possessed to the degree necessary for full autonomy, or entirely absent. The model, she claimed, sees humans as independent private actors, and relationships as 'symmetrical ones expressed by contract'.

Part of the problem she identified with applying rights to animals is the distinction between moral and legal rights. In the moral sense, rights apply everywhere and are appealed to in order to make and change laws. But, in the legal sense, contract theories see them as arising within a community, which is defined in terms of independent rational actors. While the model has its upsides, it is based on false assumptions, neglects much of what's both necessary and rewarding in life and leaves little space for notions like compassion. Justice, Midgley argued, matters most when we think about the plight of the weak and vulnerable, not when considering relations between equally powerful and articulate individuals. Rights talk encourages us to overlook vulnerability, weakness, compassion, humanity and the nonhuman world. Midgley acknowledged the attraction of extending rights to encompass nonhuman animals and recognized that rights act as powerful ideas around which to campaign.

Nevertheless, she regarded rights-talk as a poor way to describe moral obligations owed to other forms of life and to inanimate objects. Instead, Midgley argued that rights can be disentangled from duties, and that we can have a broad range of duties that exist without correlative rights. A duty, she maintained, need not indicate a contractual relationship in the way that a right sometimes seems to: 'Duties need *not* be quasi-contractual relations between symmetrical pairs of rational human agents.'[15]

There are several responses that can be made to these criticisms. While Midgley was correct that social contract theory has tended to miss something important about justice and has been based on a mistaken view of human relationships, this does not mean that it cannot be redeemed or that we should abandon the concept of rights. Work to refine social contract theory is difficult, but its fundamental ideas remain valuable: that nobody has a natural right to rule over others, and that therefore the exercise of power must be justified to those subjected to it. Much of the work in this regard is to theorize concepts like reciprocity and mutual advantage in more inclusive and expansive ways, and to design institutional structures so that they fairly represent and protect the interests of the powerless and inarticulate. While there is scope for rights-based theories to include many of the nonhuman entities Midgley thought we have duties towards, some way of distinguishing between treatment that is required and treatment that is optional is still needed. For example, Midgley's list of things we might have non-contractual duties towards includes plants of all kinds; structured objects such as crystals; places such as villages; and the dead. While these entities might be worthy of moral concern, and therefore good for us to treat with respect, they aren't the sorts of things that states ought to compel us, with threats of force, to treat in the same way as we treat those capable of suffering. Doing away with rights-talk and relying solely upon the distinctions between enforceable duties and non-enforceable duties represents little more than keeping the same structure as rights but having fewer words available to describe it.

Although the basis for her argument is quite different, there are some parallels between Midgley's critiques of rights and those made within communitarian and Marxist theories. Communitarianism is a political theory largely defined in the way it values community and opposes liberalism. For liberals, communities are valuable insofar as they contribute to the wellbeing of individuals and ensure that their rights are protected. Communitarians, however, argue that there is something valuable about community for its own sake, and that it doesn't make sense to think of individuals as separate from their community. Community is what makes us who we are; it gives us our values and our sense of identity. Liberals, they argue, mistakenly treat people as self-reliant, separate individuals and, in doing so, encourage undesirable atomistic lives. Community ought to be about the promotion of shared values more than the protection of the individual. Liberals argue that individual freedom needs to be protected from the community; communitarians argue that freedom can only be realized as part of the community. Rights, communitarians argue, are central to the liberal project and the focus on them downplays the importance of duties.

The problem with this critique is that rights are by nature relational and depend for their recognition and enforcement on a community. It isn't possible to have a system of rights without also having associated duties, so the claim that rights-talk neglects duties misunderstands the nature of rights. When communitarians make this claim, what they usually mean is that duties to community ought to take precedence over rights, which is another way of saying that rights should not protect people as much as they do, or that individuals ought to be more vulnerable to state power. The communitarian way of thinking is quite similar to certain forms of ecological ethics that place significance on ecosystems. These holistic theories are willing to sacrifice individual members of an ecological community for environmental benefits. Under this sort of approach, animals (including humans) will have a value that is connected with their contribution to an ecosystem, and this may override their individual value.

Meanwhile, the Marxist critique of rights is that they represent a system of power, designed to protect and maintain capitalist property relations, that is, the ownership by one class of people of the means by which goods are produced. Under capitalism, workers are treated as mere commodities (in Kantian terms, as mere ends rather than ends-in-themselves). From this perspective, rights embody the laws that protect the property and interests of the capitalist class. In a communist society, it is argued, humans would live according to their true nature: as cooperative social beings with shared interests. In such a world, there would be a far greater degree of freely cooperative activity, and a concern for the collective rather than individual good. Like communitarianism, this theory rejects the idea that communal interests are reducible to those of individuals. Here, the thought is that rights foster antagonistic and legalistic relationships, encouraging selfish individualism and eroding communal bonds. In a communist society there would be a concern for the collective good and people would direct themselves at shared interests, so rights would not be needed.

The Marxist critique of rights depends on several questionable assumptions. For the argument to get off the ground, the account of human nature as fundamentally cooperative and with a set of shared authentic interests and desires which will be revealed under communism must be true. However, it seems unlikely that human psychology is really like this. The idea that in the right circumstances humans will transcend the need for systems of mediation, protection from one another, and arbitration is implausible. Going beyond justice also requires a superabundance of goods, so that there is no need to compete for scarce and desirable resources, and thus no need for principles of justice governing how those goods are distributed.

In a finite world with finite resources, such an assumption is also implausible.

Nevertheless, and although Marxism has tended to be extremely anthropocentric and to disregard animal interests, a Marxist animal ethics is possible. Marxists working on animal issues have focused on the exploitation of nonhuman animals in systems of production and consumption. A Marxist animal ethics is one where nonhumans cease to be part of capitalist modes of production and are no longer regarded as products to be consumed.

Some of the criticisms in this chapter have touched on the idea that rights neglect or overlook what makes for good and rewarding lives, focusing instead on narrow sets of entitlements. However, we ought to keep in mind that the purpose of rights is not to describe everything that matters morally or to comprehensively define a good society. It is possible to have one's rights fully respected and yet nevertheless live a miserable life of boredom. It is also possible to respect another's rights for the wrong reason, and perhaps even while being a bad person. Communitarians are correct to point out that protecting rights is not the same as promoting a common good. However, they are mistaken to think that we should therefore do away with or downplay rights. Rights set out minimum standards of protection. They set the limits of what states may do to individuals in the name of the common good and they protect individuals from harm by their fellows. Rights do not tell us all that we need to live a flourishing life, merely the basic conditions that must be met before flourishing can be achieved. In the final chapter, I set out what going beyond rights, and exploring what it means to be good rather than merely to act justly towards nonhuman animals, might involve.

# 7

# CONCLUSION:
# BEYOND ANIMAL RIGHTS?

In 2015, American dentist and trophy-hunter Walter Palmer reportedly paid $50,000 (£32,000) for the opportunity to kill an endangered black-maned lion in Zimbabwe. Cecil the lion was lured out of the safety of Hwange National Park and then Palmer shot him with an arrow. Wounded, Cecil was tracked and shot with more arrows until, ten to twelve hours later and having suffered terribly, he eventually died. A month after Cecil was killed, a clothing company created a 'sexy Cecil the Lion' Halloween costume. The company claimed that 20 per cent of profits from sales would go to wildlife charities. Another company produced a Halloween costume of a dentist with a severed lion head. While Palmer can be criticized on the basis that he violated Cecil's rights, or because he caused immense suffering, most of us will probably feel uneasy or horrified about both the hunt and the costume sales in ways that go beyond rights violations and bad consequences. Indeed, from a rights perspective, the costume-makers appear to have done nothing wrong. Consequentialists might even find something praiseworthy about their actions (if they made good on their promise of donating to charity).

While animal rights are an important idea on which to campaign because they describe how nonhuman animals ought to be protected and included, they only describe part of the moral landscape. The purpose of animal rights is to make it possible for nonhuman

**Figure 7.1: Cecil the lion at Hwange National Park**

Cecil was killed for fun by a wealthy dentist hoping to use his stuffed head as a trophy. Advocates of trophy hunting often try to claim that sport hunting benefits local communities and wildlife by bringing money into deprived areas. We might wonder, if trophy hunters care as much for poor communities and wildlife as they claim, why they must cause suffering and death as a condition of their aid and what this says about their characters.

animals to live minimally decent lives, either with us or apart from us. Even though moral rights may protect the most basic interests of nonhuman animals, they don't tell us what a good life looks like. A miserable, mean-spirited person may well respect rights. Perhaps this is because they are too fearful of the consequences of violating them, or perhaps their current desires happen not to be directed at anything requiring the violation of rights. In other words, respect for moral rights is a necessary but not a sufficient condition of a good society.

Citizenship rights, briefly described in Chapter 5, go some way towards ensuring good lives, but they are only a part of the story. In Chapter 2, I introduced the ethical theory known as virtue ethics. Virtue ethicists say that rather than rights, duties and consequences, the focus of ethics should be on virtues. Virtues are settled dispositions or character traits such as kindness, humility and courage. When we possess a virtue, we are inclined to act on it without thought. An honest person doesn't need to consider if their action conforms with a norm of honesty or a duty to keep one's word before acting, they simply act honestly because that's the kind of person they are.

Recall that the ancient Greeks, along with Confucians, emphasized the relationship between treating nonhuman animals well and a person's character. Similarly, eighteenth- and nineteenth-century philosophers, campaigners and politicians fighting for better treatment of nonhumans couched their arguments in terms of the negative impacts that animal cruelty has on human psychology. One of the things virtue ethics does well is show us that morality is about more than following rules or increasing the amount of happiness in the world. Good people don't just act right and do good; they also do these things for the right *reasons* and with good motives and good intentions. If we are to think about what it means to behave as a good person, we need to consider people's attitudes and characters. Thinking in this way allows us to make sense of what is troubling in the case of poor Cecil and the companies that sought to profit from his death.

One way to think about Palmer's actions and those of the two clothing companies is that they failed to show the right sort of respect for Cecil, and for sentient life more generally. To respect something is to value it in a certain way. In respecting another being, we pay them the moral attention they deserve because we recognize their value or standing. To respect a person involves adopting an attitude that takes account of their autonomy, ruling out actions that pay no heed to their choices. Thus, paternalism is disrespectful towards autonomous agents. To respect a sentient being is to recognize that its life matters to it, and to treat it in accordance with what it wants, or would want, for itself. Respecting others involves treating them as valuable for their own sakes and holding attitudes compatible with their value. In addition to violating his rights, when Palmer killed Cecil for the fun of hunting and killing, and when he collected parts of Cecil's body to display as a trophy, he failed to show respect for him. By treating his body as a prize, Palmer showed that he regarded him as a mere thing, and by hunting him in such a painful and terrifying way, Palmer showed that he was a cruel person. He expressed vices of disrespect and cruelty.

One reply that a sport hunter might make is that Palmer showed Cecil a different kind of respect. Perhaps the hunt represented a contest of sorts, pitting the skill and patience of the hunter against the cunning and athleticism of the lion. Might we argue that Palmer, in treating Cecil as a worthy foe, showed respect for his prey?[1] Such claims are an implausible stretch. Characterizing a deliberately uneven contest, for the hunters are almost never in any danger from their prey, as a respectful hunt for a worthy opponent is risible. More likely, these arguments demonstrate either a way of rationalizing bad conduct, or the fact that the hunter regarded the animal as a means of affirming his own power and self-esteem. To require the killing of a sentient being as a way of demonstrating one's own ability shows a weakness of character rather than virtue. For companies to then make festive costumes to profit from Cecil's killing shows that they were unmoved by his pain, demonstrating the vice of callousness.

Palmer's actions, along with those of the clothing companies, demonstrated the wrong attitudes towards nonhuman animals. They expressed attitudes that contribute towards a bad and unjust world. But, if we seek a better world, what sort of character traits and attitudes towards nonhuman animals would we hope to find? What I want to do here is suggest that cultivating attitudes of respect, openness and trustworthiness towards nonhumans would not only help to secure rights and ensure societies remain just but would also make for good societies. Good societies would be those where relationships between humans and nonhumans are, in general, richer and more rewarding than they are now. I begin with the attitude of openness or acceptance before moving on to discuss the importance of being trustworthy.

In Chapter 6, I touched on the difficulty of feeling compassion for beings that are very different from us. Because part of the emotion of compassion involves trying to take the perspective of another and imagine what it feels like to be them, it can be hard to feel compassion for animals unlike ourselves. Similar problems occur with animals that we are unfamiliar with. The more we know about an animal, and the more we are exposed to them, the better we can understand their subjective experiences. Perhaps this goes some way towards explaining why animals whose lives are more visible to us tend to receive better protections in law than those kept at a distance. For nonhuman animals with physiologies and minds very different from our own, it may be that feeling compassion is impossible. It is hard to sympathize with a shark or a locust. Because of this, nonhuman animals cannot rely on our sense of compassion to protect their interests. Nevertheless, for animal rights to be secured, and then for the possibility of good interspecies relationships to be realized, people need to be motivated to respect all sentient life. Change for the better cannot happen without enough people being motivated to act; alternatives and additions to compassion are needed. One possibility is to cultivate an attitude of openness or acceptance.

Even though he excluded nonhuman animals from direct concern, Kant's work can help us here. In his writings about global politics, Kant addressed the problem of partiality, that is, that people are psychologically disposed to treat those they know favourably and to behave with suspicion, hostility or indifference towards strangers. This psychological tendency towards partiality can cause us to treat strangers unfairly and result in us failing in the moral duty to respect the humanity in all persons. Kant argued that we should develop a mindset that accepts differences and includes a willingness to engage peacefully. This mindset underpins an ethic of universal hospitality. Kant took this idea and used it to formulate principles of peacefully welcoming strangers who approach the borders of our countries. Despite being focused on human relationships, Kant's ideas can also help us think about better human–animal interactions. Because some nonhuman animals are very unlike us, we can think of them as perpetual strangers: beings whom we can never come to know well. But, if we adopt a mindset that sees beyond differences, recognizing instead that the shared capacity to suffer and be invested in our own lives places us in a common moral community, then there will be more hope for just and good relationships.[2] Attitudes of openness and acceptance allow us to live peacefully alongside others, including nonhumans, whose ways are strange and incomprehensible to us. Now that we've discussed the importance of being open and accepting towards beings quite different to us, let us finally move on to consider the value of trust.

One notable feature of human–animal relations is that humans frequently prove themselves to be untrustworthy. In Chapter 1, I showed how thousands of years of domestication have resulted in billions of nonhuman animals in our care being made dependent on us. It has also made them more vulnerable to being harmed by us. Indeed, the purpose of domestication for farmed animals is precisely that: to make them more vulnerable. Industrialized farming requires large numbers of closely housed, docile nonhuman animals. Many of the processes of rearing and husbandry aim to habituate nonhuman animals to human presence and lead those animals to expect they will not be harmed by their handlers. If cows lived in constant terror, they would be extremely difficult to transport, milk and slaughter. For farming to be efficient and safe (for farmers, at least), large animals need to trust humans. The same is true in scientific research settings, where routine medical procedures, such as drawing blood, become much more difficult and stressful if the animals do not trust their handlers.

What all this means is that humans frequently behave in ways intended to foster a sense of trust, and that they do this to make it easier to harm animals in their care. In scientific settings, primates are trained

**Figure 7.2: The farming of social animals**

Animal agriculture relies on animals that have been chosen and bred to be vulnerable and dependent on us. These animals are often reared in ways that encourage them to develop trust for their handlers. Their trust makes it easier for humans to cause them harm.

to cooperate in procedures such as venipuncture and vaginal swabbing. Venipuncture training, for blood tests and injections, involves training an animal, such as a macaque or rhesus monkey, to present part of its body voluntarily and accept venipuncture without resistance. This training reduces the stress of the animal and makes it much easier and safer for a technician. Monkeys forced to undergo the procedures involuntarily suffer serious psychological distress and exhibit a range of negative behaviours. Training begins by habituating an animal to a technician and getting them used to receiving their favourite foods from them. After that, they are trained in cages with what is known as a 'squeeze back' or 'crush cage' – a mechanism that reduces the size of the cage, forcing the animal to move to the front. Once the animal is immobilized by the squeeze back, the trainer inserts their hand and gently strokes them before grasping their leg and pulling it out of the cage opening. This process is repeated, with the animal being rewarded with treats, and then combined with venipuncture, until the monkey voluntarily presents their leg.[3] In effect, the monkeys are taught that it is safe and rewarding to present parts of their bodies, making them more vulnerable to a range of harmful procedures. Handlers deliberately foster a trusting relationship to later betray it. Similar techniques are used in farming, with systematized approaches to touching and stroking used on infant animals to foster trusting relationships in animals that will later be exploited and killed.[4]

One response to this claim is to argue that nonhuman animals are not capable of trust, so they cannot be betrayed. This is certainly true of some philosophical accounts of trust, which see the relationship as one requiring an understanding of moral concepts and involving beliefs about the values held by the object of trust. For example, such accounts hold that to trust someone to keep their promises, I must believe that they are committed to the value of promise-keeping. While these accounts certainly describe one way of trusting, they also exclude everyday understandings of trust such as between a parent and young child, carer and ward, or owner and companion animal. The kind of trust in these relationships is a feeling – an emotional bond

– that arises out of familiarity, leading to a belief that the trusted party harbours no ill intentions. Anyone who has lived with a companion animal will recognize that the process of habituation, using proximity, stroking and treats, leads in time to behaviours that bear all the hallmarks of love and affection and beliefs about the goodwill of the owner. Indeed, if our beliefs about the mental states of nonhuman animals were not reliable then we would not have been able to domesticate them in the first place.

Even if it is true that animals cannot trust in a rich sense, human handlers often see the relationships they foster as based on trust. Both the scientific literature on the handling of research animals and the accounts from farmers often describe the relationships as trusting ones. A farmer described in the *Guardian* the process of taking animals to slaughter like this:

> Raising cattle to be sold as beef is inescapably at the core of what we do, and it doesn't happen without their cooperation ... our prime cattle go straight from the field where they were born to the abattoir. The beef is sold through our local farm shop, three miles away. It's as good as it gets, and yet it presents a conflict. I am proud and fond of these steers – I bottle-fed one for many months alongside his mother, an older cow with poor milk supply – so a sense of betrayal is implicit.[5]

If humans believe themselves to have fostered trust and then go on to betray it, this says something about the trustworthiness and character of farmers and scientists.

It also tells us something about the moral quality of the processes and structures that rely on the systematic breach of trust. Even if no rights were violated, a good society is surely one in which people can trust one another. Relationships of trust are some of the most valuable. When we trust someone, we feel optimistic about their intentions, making ourselves vulnerable to being harmed and exploited. Trust makes friendship, love, democracy and basic social interaction possible. Without it, we cannot live decent lives or have decent societies. For this reason, we regard con artists and scammers are particularly egregious, because they seek out the trusting and vulnerable to serve their own ends. A betrayal of trust by a loved one is classic element of literary and cinematic tragedy because we feel the wrong so powerfully. A good person does not use trust as an instrument for their own ends. A good society for both humans and animals is one where humans behave in trustworthy ways towards the animals in their care.

If you've reached this far, thank you for sticking with me. At the start of the book, I asked you to imagine a world where humans and nonhuman animals live peacefully and well alongside one another. Over the course of the book, I have tried to show why we ought to want such a world and how rights function as an important mechanism for achieving it. The key purpose of rights is to specify the kinds of protections nonhuman animals should have, and how strong those protections should be. Rights exist to protect the most important interests of rights-holders. But rights also provide a focus and catalyst for political campaigning.

The idea of rights as a way of thinking about justice and injustice has a powerful resonance in our imagination, motivating us to make the world better and prevent wrongdoing. Even though there are difficulties in sympathizing with other animals and with applying some moral concepts to them, rights provide a way to describe the minimum standards of interspecies justice. Beyond that, they can also be used to describe how the nonhumans that are part of our political communities, and who contribute to the collective good, should be protected and compensated. Nevertheless, for all the power of rights as ethical, practical and imaginative tools, they are not the only way to think ethically about human–animal relations. Attitudes of openness, respect and trustworthiness add to the picture, giving us a vision not only of a just society for humans and animals, but also of a good and stable society. Such a world can be difficult to imagine, and even more difficult to achieve. But I believe it is one that we should hope for and one we should work towards. I hope that this book has gone some way towards persuading you of the same.

# NOTES

## Chapter 1

1   Gillian P. McHugo, Michael J. Dover and David E. MacHugh, 'Unlocking the Origins and Biology of Domestic Animals Using Ancient DNA and Paleogenomics,' *BMC Biology* 17, no. 1 (2 December, 2019), p. 98.

2   Chillingham cows weigh around 280 kg compared with an average of around 620 kg for a dairy cow in the UK.

3   Joanna Swabe, 'The Intensification of Livestock Production and The Veterinary Regime During the Twentieth Century', in Joanna Swabe (ed.) *Animals, Disease and Human Society* (Routledge, 1998).

4   Hugh LaFollette and Niall Shanks, 'Animal Experimentation: The Legacy of Claude Bernard', *International Studies in the Philosophy of Science* 8, no. 3 (1 January 1994), pp. 195–210.

5   Coral Lansbury, *The Old Brown Dog: Women, Workers and Vivisection in Edwardian England* (University of Wisconsin Press, 1985), p. 12.

6   Susan Sperling, *Animal Liberators: Research and Morality* (University of California Press, 1992), pp. 132–3.

7   Genesis 1:28.

8   Ghafir, vv. 79–80.

9   James Burgh, *The Dignity of Human Nature: Or, A Brief Account of the Certain and Established Means for Attaining the True End of Our Existence. In Four Books …* (J. Johnson and J. Payne, 1767), p. 78; Carol J. Adams, *The Sexual Politics of Meat: A Feminist-Vegetarian Critical Theory*, 20th Anniversary Edition, Revised (Bloomsbury Academic, 2010).

10   William Youatt, *The Obligation and Extent of Humanity to Brutes: Principally Considered with Reference to the Domesticated Animals* (Longman, Orme, Brown, Green, and Longman, 1839), p. 32.

11   Peter Singer, 'All Animals Are Equal', in Peter Singer (ed.), *Applied Ethics*, Oxford Readings in Philosophy (Oxford University Press, 1986), p. 220.
12   Protection of Animals Act 1911.
13   Animal Welfare (Sentience) Act 2022.

## Chapter 2

1    Kevin Blankinship, 'Suffering the Sons of Eve: Animal Ethics in al-Ma'arri's Epistle of the Horse and the Mule', *Religions* 11, no. 8 (August 2020): 8, https://doi.org/10.3390/rel11080412
2    Reynold A. Nicholson, *Studies in Islamic Poetry*, Reissue edition (Cambridge University Press, 2011).
3    D.S. Margoliouth, 'Art. XI.—Abu'l-'Alā al- Ma'arri's Correspondence on Vegetarianism', *Journal of the Royal Asiatic Society* 34, no. 2 (April 1902), p. 317.
4    Margoliouth, p. 321.
5    The term 'vegetarianism' came into use after the incorporation of the Vegetarian Society in Ramsgate in 1847.
6    Antonio Cocchi, *The Pythagorean Diet, of Vegetables Only, Conducive to the Preservation of Health, and the Cure of Diseases* (R. Dodsley, 1745), p. 28.
7    Cicero, Jonathan Powell, and Niall Rudd, *The Republic and The Laws*, Reissue edition (Oxford University Press, 2008), p. 64.
8    Aristotle, *The Art of Rhetoric*, ed. Harvey Yunis (Oxford University Press, 2018), p. 50. The comparison Aristotle makes is between Empedocles on killing animals and Sophocles' Antigone, who describes burying her brother as an act of justice even though King Creon has forbidden it. Aristotle's point is that good conduct and lawful conduct are not always the same.
9    Marcus Tullius Cicero, *Cicero: On Moral Ends* (Cambridge University Press, 2001), sec. 3.67.
10   John Rawls, *A Theory of Justice: Revised Edition* (Belknap Press of Harvard University Press, 1999), p. 448.
11   Mary Midgley, 'Duties Concerning Islands', in Robert Elliot (ed.) *Environmental Ethics*, Reprint edition (Oxford University Press, 1995), pp. 89–103.
12   Porphyry, *Select Works of Porphyry: Containing His Four Books On Abstinence from Animal Food; His Treatise On the Homeric Cave of the Nymphs; and His Auxiliaries to the Perception of Intelligible Natures*, trans. Thomas Taylor (Thomas Rodd, 1823), p. 104.

13   M.F. Burnyeat, *Explorations in Ancient and Modern Philosophy*, vol. 2 (Cambridge University Press, 2012), ch. 14, https://doi.org/10.1017/CBO9780511974069

14   Neoplatonism was a Greco-Roman school of thought that existed between the third and seventh centuries CE.

15   Mencius 1A:7, quoted in Ruiping Fan, 'How Should We Treat Animals? A Confucian Reflection', *Dao* 9, no. 1 (1 March 2010), pp. 84–5.

16   Donald N. Blakeley, 'Listening to the Animals: The Confucian View of Animal Welfare', *Journal of Chinese Philosophy* 30, no. 2 (2003), p. 144.

17   Montaigne, *The Complete Essays of Montaigne*, trans. Donald Frame (Stanford University Press, 1958), pp. 317–18.

18   Montaigne, p. 358.

19   Jean-Jacques Rousseau, *Discourse on the Origin of Inequality*, ed. Patrick Coleman, trans. Franklin Philip (Oxford University Press, 2009), p. 18.

20   The observant reader will have spotted Rousseau's reference to 'the ancient dispute about the participation of animals in natural law'. His comments later in the *Discourse* show that the 'ancient dispute' does not refer to the Romans. However, we do know that his thinking on nonhuman animals was influenced by the ancient Greeks and that his favourite author as a child was Plutarch. Thus, the most likely explanation is that the ancient dispute Rousseau refers to is that between ancient Greek thinkers, and that he has mistaken claims about virtue and good character for arguments about natural law.

21   Jean-Jacques Rousseau, *Emile, or, On Education: Includes Emile and Sophie, or, The Solitaries*, ed. and trans. Allan Bloom and Christopher Kelly (Dartmouth College Press, 2010), p. 297.

22   Mary Wollstonecraft, *A Vindication of the Rights of Men; A Vindication of the Rights of Woman; An Historical and Moral View of the French Revolution*, ed. Janet Todd, Reissue edition (Oxford University Press, 2008), p. 258.

23   See, for example: Charlie Robinson and Victoria Clausen, 'The Link Between Animal Cruelty and Human Violence', *FBI: Law Enforcement Bulletin*, 10 August 2021, https://leb.fbi.gov/articles/featured-articles/the-link-between-animal-cruelty-and-human-violence

24 Immanuel Kant, *Kant: Groundwork of the Metaphysics of Morals*, ed. Jens Timmermann, trans. Mary Gregor, 2nd edition (Cambridge University Press, 2012), sec. 4:429.

25 Immanuel Kant, *Lectures on Ethics* (Harper & Row, 1963), pp. 239–41.

26 In a similar vein, in 1792 Thomas Taylor published *A Vindication of the Rights of Brutes* as a mockery of Mary Wollstonecraft's *A Vindication of the Rights of Women*.

27 S.M. Okin, *Women in Western Political Thought*, Reprint edition (Princeton University Press, 1992).

28 Carol J. Adams, *The Sexual Politics of Meat – 25th Anniversary Edition: A Feminist-Vegetarian Critical Theory* (Bloomsbury Academic, 2015).

29 Jeremy Bentham, *An Introduction to the Principles of Morals and Legislation* (Printed for W. Pickering, 1823), p. 311.

30 Bentham, p. 310.

31 Peter Singer, 'The Fable of the Fox and the Unliberated Animals', *Ethics* 88, no. 2 (1978): pp. 119–25.

32 Judith Norman, Alistair Welchman and Christopher Janaway (eds), *Schopenhauer: 'The World as Will and Representation'*, trans. Judith Norman and Alistair Welchman, vol. 1, The Cambridge Edition of the Works of Schopenhauer (Cambridge University Press, 2010), pp. 399–400n.

33 Arthur Schopenhauer, *On the Basis of Morality: Translated by E. F. J. Payne; with An Introduction by Richard Taylor* (Bobbs-Merrill, 1965), pp. 175–6.

34 Schopenhauer, *On the Basis of Morality*, p. 96.

35 Arthur Schopenhauer, *Schopenhauer: Parerga and Paralipomena: Short Philosophical Essays*, ed. Adrian Del Caro and Christopher Janaway, trans. Adrian Del Caro, vol. 2, The Cambridge Edition of the Works of Schopenhauer (Cambridge University Press, 2015), p. 337.

36 Frances Power Cobbe, 'The Rights of Man and the Claims of Brutes', *Fraser's Magazine for Town and Country, 1830–1869* 68, no. 407 (November 1863), pp. 586–602.

37 Robert Nozick, *Anarchy, State, and Utopia* (Basic Books, 1974), p. 39.

38 Frances Power Cobbe, *The Modern Rack; Papers on Vivisection* (Sonnenschein, 1889), p. 32.

39 Adams, *The Sexual Politics of Meat*, ch. 9.

[40] M.K. Gandhi, *An Autobiography or the Story of My Experiments with Truth: A Critical Edition*, trans. Mahadev Desai (Yale University Press, 2018), Pt. 1, chapter XV.

## Chapter 3

[1] Also known as the argument from marginal cases or the argument from species overlap.

[2] Larry Sumner, *The Moral Foundation of Rights* (Oxford University Press, 1989), p. 47.

[3] Joseph Raz, *The Morality of Freedom* (Oxford University Press, 1988), ch. 7.

[4] Steve Cooke, 'The Ethics of Touch and the Importance of Nonhuman Relationships in Animal Agriculture', *Journal of Agricultural and Environmental Ethics* 34, no. 2 (1 April 2021), p. 12.

[5] Steve Cooke, 'Animal Kingdoms: On Habitat Rights for Wild Animals,' *Environmental Values* 26, no. 1 (February 2017), pp. 53–72.

[6] John Rawls, *A Theory of Justice: Revised Edition* (Belknap Press of Harvard University Press, 1999), p. 4.

## Chapter 4

[1] Kelly Anthis and Jacy Reese Anthis, 'Global Farmed & Factory Farmed Animals Estimates', last updated 21 February 2019, https://sentienceinstitute.org/global-animal-farming-estimates

[2] Faunalytics estimate the global figure for chickens at 97 per cent factory farmed, see: https://faunalytics.org/fundamentals-farmed-animals/

[3] Olga G. Pyankova et al., 'Isolation of Clade 2.3.4.4b A(H5N8), a Highly Pathogenic Avian Influenza Virus, from a Worker during an Outbreak on a Poultry Farm, Russia, December 2020', *Eurosurveillance* 26, no. 24 (17 June 2021): 2100439.

[4] Gary L. Francione, 'Animals as Property', *Animal Law* 2 (1996), p. i.

[5] Isaiah Berlin, *Four Essays on Liberty* (Oxford University Press, 1969), p. xliii.

[6] For an argument along these lines see A. Cochrane, 'Do Animals Have an Interest in Liberty?', *Political Studies*, 57, no. 3 (2009), pp. 660–79.

7   S. Monsó, J. Benz-Schwarzburg and A. Bremhorst, 'Animal
    Morality: What It Means and Why It Matters'. *J Ethics* 22 (2018),
    pp. 283–310.

8   Douglas-Hamilton, I. et al. 'Behavioural Reactions of Elephants
    Towards a Dying and Deceased Matriarch', *Applied Animal
    Behaviour Science*, 100, no. 1 (2006) , pp. 87–102.

9   Kristin Andrews, *The Animal Mind: An Introduction to the
    Philosophy of Animal Cognition*, 2nd edition (Routledge, 2020),
    p. 97.

10  *Matter of Nonhuman Rights Project, Inc. v. Breheny* 2022 NY Slip
    Op 03859.

11  Harry F. Harlow and Margaret Kuenne Harlow, 'Social
    Deprivation in Monkeys', *Scientific American* 207, no. 5 (1962),
    p. 138.

12  William Moy Stratton Russell and Rex Leonard Burch, *The
    Principles of Humane Experimental Technique* (Methuen, 1959).

## Chapter 5

1   Donald Broom, 'Fish Brains and Behaviour Indicate Capacity for
    Feeling Pain', *Animal Sentience* 1, no. 3 (1 January 2016).

2   Lynne Sneddon et al., 'Fish Sentience Denial: Muddying the
    Waters', *Animal Sentience* 3, no. 21 (1 January 2018).

3   Robyn J. Crook, 'Behavioral and Neurophysiological Evidence
    Suggests Affective Pain Experience in Octopus', *iScience* 24, no. 3
    (19 March 2021): 102229.

4   Andrew Crump et al., 'Sentience in Decapod Crustaceans: A
    General Framework and Review of the Evidence', *Animal Sentience*
    7, no. 32 (1 January 2022), https://doi.org/10.51291/2377-
    7478.1691

5   Colin Klein and Andrew Barron, 'Insects Have the Capacity for
    Subjective Experience', *Animal Sentience* 1, no. 9 (11 July 2016).

6   Matilda Gibbons et al., 'Motivational Trade-Offs and Modulation
    of Nociception in Bumblebees', *Proceedings of the National
    Academy of Sciences* 119, no. 31 (2 August 2022): e2205821119.

7   Jonathan Birch, 'Animal Sentience and the Precautionary Principle',
    *Animal Sentience*, 2, no. 6 (2017).

8   Tom Regan, *The Case for Animal Rights*, 2nd edition (University of
    California Press, 2004), p. 361.

9   Damian Carrington, 'Humans Just 0.01% of All Life but Have
    Destroyed 83% of Wild Mammals – Study', *Guardian*, 21 May
    2018, https://www.theguardian.com/environment/2018/may/21/

human-race-just-001-of-all-life-but-has-destroyed-over-80-of-wild-mammals-study

10   Sue Donaldson and Will Kymlicka, *Zoopolis: A Political Theory of Animal Rights* (Oxford University Press, 2011).


## Chapter 6

1   James Jasper and Dorothy Nelkin, *The Animal Rights Crusade: The Growth of a Moral Protest* (The Free Press, 1991), ch. 7.

2   This phenomenon is known as negativity bias.

3   Paul Lucardie, 'Animalism: A Nascent Ideology? Exploring the Ideas of Animal Advocacy Parties', *Journal of Political Ideologies* 25, no. 2 (3 May 2020), pp. 212–27.

4   Peter Singer, *Animal Liberation: Towards an End to Man's Inhumanity to Animals* (Granada Publishing, 1977), p. 9.

5   See Michele M. Moody-Adams, 'The Idea of Moral Progress', *Metaphilosophy* 30, no. 3 (1999), pp. 168–85; Martha Nussbaum, 'On Moral Progress: A Response to Richard Rorty', *The University of Chicago Law Review* 74, no. 3 (2007), pp. 953–4.

6   Ruth Byrne, *The Rational Imagination: How People Create Alternatives to Reality* (MIT Press, 2007).

7   S. Cooke 'Imagined Utopias: Animals Rights and the Moral Imagination,' *Journal of Political Philosophy*, 25, no. 4 (2017), pp. e1–e18.

8   This gulf in subjective experiences can also pose problems for identifying the interests of nonhuman animals and thus the rights they ought to possess.

9   Peter Singer, *The Expanding Circle – Ethics, Evolution, and Moral Progress*, Edition with a new afterword by the author (Princeton University Press, 2011), pp. 119–20.

10   Cara C. MacInnis and Gordon Hodson, 'It Ain't Easy Eating Greens: Evidence of Bias toward Vegetarians and Vegans from Both Source and Target', *Group Processes & Intergroup Relations* 20, no. 6 (1 November 2017), pp. 721–44.

11   For a real-life example, see: https://aeon.co/essays/how-a-change-for-the-worse-makes-for-a-different-person

12   MacInnis and Hodson, 'It Ain't Easy Eating Greens'.

13   Richard Twine, 'Vegan Killjoys at the Table: Contesting Happiness and Negotiating Relationships with Food Practices,' *Societies* 4, no. 4 (December 2014), pp. 623–39.

14     Mary Midgley, 'Duties Concerning Islands', in Robert Elliot (ed.) *Environmental Ethics*, Reprint edition (Oxford University Press, 1995), pp. 89–103.
15     Midgley, 'Duties Concerning Islands', p. 101.

## Chapter 7

1     See, for example, D. Demetriou and B. Fischer, 'Dignitarian Hunting: A Rights-based Defense,' *Social Theory and Practice*, 44, no. 1 (2018), pp. 49–73.
2     Steve Cooke, 'Perpetual Strangers: Animals and the Cosmopolitan Right', *Political Studies*, 62, no. 4 (2014), pp. 930–44.
3     V. Reinhart, 'Training Adult Male Rhesus Monkeys to Actively Cooperate During In-Homecage Venipuncture. *Anim. Technol.*, 42 (1991), pp. 11–17.
4     S. Cooke (2021) 'The Ethics of Touch and the Importance of Nonhuman Relationships in Animal Agriculture', *Journal of Agricultural and Environmental Ethics*, 34, no. 2 (2021), p. 12.
5     S. Laughton, 'Country Diary: I'm Fond of These Steers. Today Feels Like a Betrayal', *Guardian*, 15 August 2022. Available at: https://www.theguardian.com/environment/2022/aug/15/country-diary-im-fond-of-these-steers-today-feels-like-a-betrayal

# FURTHER READING

Carol J. Adams, *The Sexual Politics of Meat –
25th Anniversary Edition: A Feminist-Vegetarian
Critical Theory* (Bloomsbury Academic, 2015).

Alasdair Cochrane, *Should Animals Have Political
Rights?* (Polity, 2019).

J.M. Coetzee, *Elizabeth Costello* (Penguin, 2004).

Eva Meijer, *When Animals Speak: Toward an Interspecies
Democracy* (New York University Press, 2019).

Mary Midgley, *Animals and Why They Matter* (University
of Georgia Press, 1983).

Tony Milligan, *Beyond Animal Rights: Food, Pets and
Ethics* (Continuum, 2010).

Martha C. Nussbaum, *Justice for Animals: Our Collective
Responsibility* (Simon & Schuster, 2023).

David M. Peña-Guzmán, *When Animals Dream: The
Hidden World of Animal Consciousness* (Princeton
University Press, 2022).

Peter Singer, *Animal Liberation: Towards an End to Man's
Inhumanity to Animals* (Granada Publishing, 1977).

# INDEX

Page numbers in *italics* refer to figures
and those in **bold** refer to boxes